FRATERNITY

FRATERNITY

Diane Brady

SPIEGEL & GRAU

NEW YORK

2012

Published in the United States by Spiegel & Grau, an imprint of The Random House Publishing Group, a division of Random House, Inc., New York.

SPIEGEL & GRAU and design is a registered trademark of Random House, Inc.

Photograph on p. 111 courtesy of Arthur Martin; photographs pages 151, 197, and 206 courtesy of Theodore V. Wells. All other photographs in this book are courtesy of the College of the Holy Cross Archives.

Library of Congress Cataloging-in-Publication Data

Brady, Diane.
Fraternity / Diane Brady.
p.   cm.
ISBN 978-0-385-52474-2
eBook ISBN 978-0-385-52962-4
1. Brooks, John E.   2. Educators—United States.   3. College of the Holy Cross (Worcester, Mass.)—Alumni and alumnae.   4. African American men—Education (Higher)   5. African American male college students.   6. College integration—United States.   7. Successful people—United States.   I. Title.
LA2317.B578A3 2012
378'.07209251—dc23   2011023764

Printed in the United States of America on acid-free paper

www.spiegelandgrau.com

9 8 7 6 5 4 3 2 1

First Edition

Book design by Caroline Cunningham

To Father Brooks, who has inspired generations of Holy Cross students. To Barry, for giving me space, time, and guidance. And to Elliott, Natalie, and Connor, for all their laughter and love.

CONTENTS

INTRODUCTION

I first heard of the Reverend John E. Brooks, S.J., in late 2005, when I was a senior writer at *BusinessWeek*. I was having lunch at a midtown Manhattan restaurant with a PR executive named Eric Starkman and his client Stan Grayson, a lawyer and former deputy mayor of New York who was then president of one of the country's few minority-owned investment banks, M.R. Beal & Company. It was really just a courtesy meeting; I rarely covered Wall Street, but I trusted Eric's judgment about people, and he said Grayson was a man I should take the time to meet. Over lunch, the three of us chatted about the economy, basketball, and how New York had changed since Grayson oversaw its finances during the 1980s. The conversation turned to Ted Wells, a lawyer who had been profiled in a *New York Times* article that week. Wells was representing Scooter Libby, the senior aide to Vice President Dick Cheney who'd been charged with perjury and obstruction of justice for allegedly leaking the identity of CIA officer Valerie Plame to the media. It seemed natural that Libby would turn to Wells, who had a record of representing high-profile defendants, including junk bond king Michael Milken, former agriculture secretary Mike Espy, tobacco giant Philip Morris, and Exxon Mobil, and who would later go on to represent Eliot Spitzer. The *Times* article had painted Wells as a formidable trial lawyer—"one of the best" in the country—who had been raised by a single mother in Washington, D.C., and had attended college on a football scholarship.

It turned out that Wells and Grayson had attended the College of the Holy Cross in Worcester, Massachusetts, together. Grayson recalled that Wells had shared a dorm room with Eddie Jenkins, who became a running back with the Miami Dolphins during the team's legendary 1972 perfect season and went on to establish his own law practice before becoming chairman of the Massachusetts Alcoholic Beverages Control Commission. Down the hall from them, Grayson said, was the writer Edward P. Jones, who would later win a MacArthur Foundation "genius" grant and a Pulitzer Prize for his novel *The Known World*. Another hallmate was future Supreme Court justice Clarence Thomas.

They had all arrived on campus in the fall of 1968, at a time when the civil rights of African Americans had taken on a new urgency amid the rise of the black power movement and the assassination of Dr. Martin Luther King, Jr., earlier that year, in April. The passage of the Civil Rights Act of 1964 and the Voting Rights Act a year later had fostered both hope and frustration: hope that black Americans would finally experience the same rights and opportunities as everyone else, and frustration that the progress was so slow. One of the most obvious signs of inequality was the higher education system. While public schools had started to desegregate in the 1950s, many of the nation's top colleges remained bastions of white privilege well over a decade later. They had been slow to open their doors to black students, and even slower to reach out to them with scholarships and support. Racial integration may have been a topic of debate on college campuses by 1968, but evidence of it was still in short supply. To have such an accomplished group of African American men emerge from a small Irish Catholic college in central Massachusetts seemed both unusual and amazing.

"Was there something in the water?" I joked. Grayson shook his head and said, "It was Father Brooks." He went on to describe a compassionate, if sometimes brusque, priest who mentored, defended, coached, and befriended the group of black students who were at Holy Cross in the late 1960s. He'd personally had a hand in recruiting them to the school and had pushed to get the money for full scholarships at a time when many of his peers were unsure about whether to seek out minority students. He'd then nurtured them through their often challenging years at Holy Cross. When all of the black students at the college had quit school in protest against alleged racism in 1969, Brooks had been the one to bring them back. When the students needed supplies, transportation, and a place where they could live together and create a community on the otherwise white campus, Brooks had come through with the money or authorization needed to make it happen. It was less the material support, though, than the knowledge that he believed in the young men and had their backs. Without Brooks, Grayson insisted, "none of us would have made it."

I asked Grayson when he had last been in touch with the priest, expecting to hear another anecdote from the early 1970s. The answer, "a few weeks ago," surprised me. Since the men had graduated, Brooks had remained involved in their lives—standing up for Thomas in his bid for the Supreme Court, calling members of the group to celebrate accomplishments, presiding over weddings and the occasional funeral. Decades after they had left the school, many of the men had continued to gather at Wells's house for an annual barbecue. The college friends were godfathers to one another's children.

Naturally, I was curious. In the months and years that followed, I met with Brooks and the men whose lives he had influenced. In addition to Wells, Thomas, Jones, Grayson, and Jenkins, other talented young black men mentored by Father Brooks had gone on to build successful careers in law, business, and other areas. One became a prominent physician who served on Air Force Two; another spent two seasons in the NFL. The story was not entirely a triumphant one: Of the twenty black men who arrived at Holy Cross in the fall of 1968—nineteen freshmen and Thomas, who had transferred to the school as a sophomore—only a dozen would make it to graduation. Some got distracted by drugs, politics, and the lure of life outside of the classroom. Some dropped out, or were kicked out. Still, a number of them thrived spectacularly, both at Holy Cross and in the world at large.

Though they came of age during an era that Reverend Jesse Jackson described to me as one marked by "warmth toward social justice from the top," the men's success was not merely a product of the times. Even Ted Wells, who identifies strongly with the larger generational movement that pushed for everything from racial integration to ending the Vietnam War, marvels at the accomplishments of the small, tight-knit group. "Sometimes I think it could have been serendipity," Wells told me. "I like to think it's something more—some combination of us and Father Brooks and other people we met during this incredible time in history."

To me there seemed to be a powerful story behind Wells's breezy assessment. The black recruits' experiences raised important questions about the role that one man could play in altering the lives of those around him, even as he struggled to meet competing demands. I was also intrigued by the influence that the men had on one another, and on the middle-aged Jesuit who knew little about the African American experience. I wanted to learn more about the individual experiences of these men during a formative period in their development, a period that's often subject to revisionist history later in life. Memories of college can come to take on a golden aura or can be cast aside in disdain once they're at odds with a person's new life script. The moments of bitterness or joy can become exaggerated, while perceptions about the influences of particular events or people are apt to change.

To read the memoirs of Justice Clarence Thomas, for example, is to learn about a Holy Cross experience that's abbreviated and seems somewhat diminished—a chapter in which an angry rebel ultimately comes to his senses and manages to distance himself from his radicalized peers. To talk to Thomas in person, though, is to listen to a man whose loud laugh and obvious fondness for his former classmates suggest a more nuanced experience during those years in Worcester. Some classmates recall a more studious or sullen side of Thomas; others remember the jokes, the debates, and the camaraderie. What Thomas doesn't dispute is where he found help in getting through a tough period. To him, there's no surprise in the successes of Ted Wells, Stan Grayson, and Ed Jones. It wasn't serendipity that his peers went on to have such successful careers, he told me. "It was Father Brooks."

What follows is the story of five of those men who met during a transformative period in U.S. history, men who were eager to embrace new opportunities being offered even as they voiced anger at what was still being denied. They were an unfamiliar force at an all-male college that, like many other schools in the late 1960s, was struggling to hold on to its traditions while trying to adapt to new realities. And they were influenced by a Boston-born Jesuit who, besides changing their lives, was himself forever changed by this first group of black recruits to come to Holy Cross.

ONE

All of King's Men

On April 4, 1968, eight black students were enrolled at the College of the Holy Cross. One, an outgoing and opinionated sophomore named Arthur "Art" Martin, from Newark, New Jersey, was studying in his dorm's common room when he heard a commotion in the hall. A white student ran in and announced to everyone present that "Martin Luther Coon" had been shot. He looked Art straight in the eye, as if daring him to acknowledge the slur. There was an uncomfortable silence in the room as the other students all turned to stare, curious to see how the black student was going to react to the news of the civil rights leader's death. Art calmly got up and left the study area. He held his composure until he found his friend Orion Douglass, a black senior from Savannah, and only then did his tears start to flow.

About 1,400 miles away, at the Immaculate Conception Seminary, a young student was battling his rage. Conception, Missouri, was no place to mourn the death of a black man. Clarence Thomas knew he didn't fit in. From the minute he had arrived from Georgia in the tiny rural community where he had come to study for the priesthood, he'd had misgivings that were increasingly hard to ignore. Thomas had promised his grandfather that he would become the first black priest in Savannah, and he knew that the consequences of letting down the man who had raised him would be dire. His grandfather had made it clear that if Thomas dropped out of school, he would not be welcome back home. Thomas hadn't expected to have fun in Missouri—he wasn't the type of teenager who put having a good time ahead of an education—but the isolation and loneliness

Clarence Thomas

he experienced was a shock. While Thomas may have come across as friendly and enthusiastic to his fellow seminarians—three of whom were black—he had privately come to loathe his life at the pastoral theology school. Though he liked quite a few of his peers, he felt he had little in common with them. They sometimes stared at his black skin and spoke disparagingly about men like Martin Luther King, Jr., and Malcolm X. The biggest problem, though, wasn't the other men but the demons he was battling within himself. Thomas had been mourning the death of a friend who had been killed in a fight in Savannah, and had been reading about the philosophies of a new generation of black leaders.

That sorrow, combined with the racial tensions he felt at the seminary, had merely added to his doubts about why he was there. The Roman Catholic Church had once seemed like a sanctuary from racism to Thomas. The Franciscan sisters who had taught him at St. Benedict the Moor Grammar School had shown him a level of respect he had rarely encountered on the streets of Savannah. Even St. John Vianney Minor Seminary, a white boarding school near Savannah where he had finished up high school and endured occasional teasing, had been at least tolerable in his mind. But a lot had changed over the past year. Civil rights activists like Stokeley Carmichael and Bobby Seale had helped to make black power a rallying cry on campuses nationwide, instilling black students with both a sense of pride and anger about social injustice. There was a growing sense across the country that it was time to give African Americans the rights they had been denied for so long. But one institution that had yet to come to that conclusion, in Thomas's view, was the Roman Catholic Church. Despite the bold and inclusive vision of Catholicism that emerged from the Second Vatican Council, or Vatican II, he saw hypocrisy in where the Church was spending its energies. Thomas found that the Church's discussions about how to become more relevant were lacking any real focus on the evils of racism, or on the racial segregation within the Church hierarchy. Thomas had once believed that becoming a priest would put him on equal footing with his white peers; now he wasn't so sure. With each passing day, he instead felt more diminished and full of doubt.

Even as he gave the appearance of fitting in, Thomas felt left out by the conversations that seemed to grow quieter when he entered a room, the choice of TV shows in common areas, and even the letters that other students received from parents who seemed to care about their sons in a way that his own mother and father never had. His father had left the family when Clarence was a toddler, while his mother had left her two boys with their grandfather when Thomas was barely seven.

The scripture Thomas studied felt out of sync with the realities of 1968. The men living in Conception seemed to him oblivious to a world that was exploding with images of war, protests, and injustice. Instead of acting as a catalyst in the push for racial equality, the Church seemed to have become an oasis from it. It was hard for him to keep his faith when, amid all the battles and debates and violence over civil rights, the Church said nothing. As he would say years later, the silence haunted him.

Martin Luther King, Jr., was a beacon of hope for Thomas; through his work, King had helped him to articulate the pain he felt at being black in a racist world, a pain that Thomas had worked hard to ignore most of his life. The only time he had really been unaware of it was in the small black community of Pin Point, Georgia, where he had lived until the age of six. After his younger brother, Myers, accidentally burned down the house where they lived, the boys had moved to the slums of Savannah with their mother while Thomas's older sister stayed in Pin Point with another relative.

On the evening of April 4, Thomas was walking back to his dormitory when one of the men watching TV suddenly yelled that King had been shot. As Thomas stood there, trying to digest the news, he heard a white classmate say, "That's good. I hope the son of a bitch dies." The man who'd said he hoped King would die was a future priest. In that moment, all of the white students seemed the same to Thomas. Just as King had given voice to Thomas's hopes, one wisecracking student brought clarity to his anger. It was apparent to him that he didn't belong with these men. There was no sanctuary in the Church, no equality in Catholicism for people like him. Thomas no longer felt a desire to swallow his rage and head off to the chapel to pray. He simply made a decision, then and there, to leave the seminary and never come back. Later in life, Thomas would refer back to King's death as a turning point, as the moment when he abandoned both his faith and his vocation.

At seventeen, Eddie Jenkins had a confidence that many adults envied. He was handsome, in an approachable sort of way, and had a reputation for being charming and funny. His days were filled with commuting more than two hours to school and football practice in Brooklyn before returning to Queens and his after-school job at Alexander's department store. On April 4, Jenkins was stocking shelves at Alexander's when he looked up to see an older black man walking slowly toward him. What an Uncle Tom, the teen thought to himself. The low hang of the stranger's head gave the man the kind of look that men his father's age sometimes had, as if they had spent so much of their lives bowing to white people that they had forgotten how to stand tall. Jenkins turned away in disgust and went back to his work, absently wondering why the street outside wasn't buzzing with its usual mix of music, laughter, and the chatter of commuters.

Eddie Jenkins

As the man approached him, Jenkins grudgingly asked if he needed help.

"The king is dead," the man said.

Jenkins saw tears in the man's eyes and suddenly understood why he looked so beaten down. Martin Luther King, Jr., was dead. The teen was overcome with shock. But his most overwhelming reaction was shame—shame that he had stereotyped a grieving man as a coward.

The man looked straight into Jenkins's eyes. "You can go home now," he said. The statement struck him as surprisingly bold, but Jenkins immediately went to the register and cashed out. When he turned around, the man was gone. Once outside, he realized again how quiet the streets were. In other parts of the city, people were already smashing store windows and setting fires, but on Queens Boulevard it seemed like the world had stopped. The few people who were still milling around were walking in silence, trying to absorb King's death. When Jenkins got home to the Flushing section of Queens known as "Da'Ville," his family was gathered in the living room.

"It had to be a white man," his father said, looking up from the TV. Eddie's father was a former merchant marine with a strong gut instinct. It was a trait that had enabled him to form the neighborhood's first boys' baseball team when Eddie was ten, soliciting hand-me-down uniforms from the local Jewish league and inviting white boys who hadn't made the cut elsewhere. The team won the league championships in its first year, and Jenkins's father went on to become league commissioner. No one knew yet who had killed King, but there was no doubt in Eddie's father's voice. Moreover, everyone else in the room was equally convinced that he was right.

At that moment, all of the speeches Eddie had heard from his father about learning to work with white people felt meaningless. The world was divided again. Eddie thought there was no way that black America would let this man die without some kind of retribution. He wanted to rush outside to see what was happening, but his parents convinced him to stay in the house. He had too much to lose, they said—the chance at a football scholarship, college, a lucrative career. None of those things would come to someone who was caught participating in violent demonstrations. Eddie obediently sat down in the living room and stared numbly at the TV.

Years later, after Jenkins and his Miami Dolphins had won the 1972 Super Bowl and he had moved from the NFL to become a politically active lawyer and chairman of the Massachusetts Alcoholic Beverages Control Commission, he would still cite King's death as a turning point in his life. The civil rights battles that had seemed somewhat abstract up to that point suddenly felt personal.

By the age of seventeen, Edward Paul Jones had given up on the idea of real friendship. He and his family had already moved eighteen times around their poor northwest neighborhood in Washington, D.C. What had stayed consistent, he would later recall, were the rats and rent collectors that seemed to follow them to each new location. On the night of April 4, Jones was where he usually was at that time of day, at home, sitting alone and reading a book.

Edward P. Jones

His mother was washing dishes, cleaning floors, and peeling potatoes at a French restaurant called Chez François in the center of town. His father had left long ago, when Ed was two and his mother was pregnant with her third child. Jones's sister, now fifteen, had moved up to Brooklyn a few years earlier to live with an aunt, and his sixteen-year-old brother was living in a "children's village" in Laurel, Maryland, about twenty miles outside Washington. Jones vividly remembered the day his mother had to confront the reality that her middle child had come into the world with a brain that, as he would later put it, didn't work quite right. Jones was four years old when a letter arrived. Unable to read or write, his mother had wandered through the boardinghouse where they lived, trying to find someone to read it. When she finally found a man on his way up the stairs, he told her that the note was from a city court, warning her that officials were coming to take Joseph away because he was "feeble-minded." Jeanette had collapsed on the stairs in tears, clutching her daughter as Ed just watched and felt alone.

Now it was just Ed and his mother, living together but largely keeping out of each other's way. He had turned off the evening news earlier than usual, thus missing the special bulletin that announced King's assassination. Jones didn't learn about King's death until the next morning, when he turned on the radio. He and his mother sat in silence. Neither of them had ever paid much attention to the civil rights leader. His mother had been too busy keeping up with the demands of life to let herself get wrapped up in dreaming about civil rights. For her bookish son, the idea that King's fight might become his own seemed equally remote.

By the time Jones went outside, he smelled smoke and stepped over broken glass—evidence of the rioting that had begun during the night. He was barely a block from home when a black man walked by, struggling with a television in his arms. A group of white men came up behind him and confiscated it. They looked official, wearing what appeared to be something akin to police uniforms, but there was something in the way they laughed when they grabbed the TV set that made Jones think they were just robbers in another guise.

Jones wandered the streets surveying the destruction. When he came up to a Hahn Shoes store he had passed every day, he stopped. The windows were broken and people were streaming onto the streets with as many shoe boxes as they could carry. Jones felt himself drawn inside, where his eyes watered from what he assumed must have been tear gas. His eyes fell on a display of twenty-dollar shoes, and he quickly pulled out a pair that seemed to be his size and ran out. They would be good shoes for college, he decided.

Although he performed well at school, Jones didn't know much about his chances for college. He had looked at Howard University, but just applying there would have meant paying extra money to take the relatively new ACT college entrance exam in addition to the usual SAT test, so he had ruled it out. And he was nowhere near the top of the list at the new Federal City College, which seemed to be accepting everybody. He was no athlete, either. He hadn't even done particularly well on the SAT. But a few months earlier, a young Jesuit who knew him from the neighborhood had told him about Holy Cross, where a priest named John Brooks was eager to recruit black students. The priest told Jones that Brooks might drive him to the campus for a weekend if Jones could get a bus to Philadelphia and meet up with some other students. Jones decided to follow up on the offer. As he grabbed the shoes, he was thinking about wearing them to Worcester.

Stanley Grayson was enjoying his status as a minor celebrity. The basketball team at All Saints High School in Detroit had recently won the state championships for the first time in its history, and many gave Grayson the credit. With just seconds left and a one-point lead in the final game, Grayson had been fouled and sank both his shots to seal a victory. The six-foot-four team captain was suddenly a hero. The city's Catholic High School

Stanley Grayson

League named him outstanding scholar-athlete of the year. He was getting scholarship offers from schools that included Villanova and the University of Michigan. Having also helped his team finish as runner-up in the state championships the year before, Grayson didn't have to worry about anyone doubting his skills. Whatever discomfort he may have felt at being black in a school full of Hungarian and Polish kids was outweighed by the reality that, at the moment, he was a star.

Grayson didn't have many complaints. He couldn't recall a time when he'd ever felt underprivileged. Detroit had been the site of a racial inferno a year earlier, but it wasn't the same hotbed of inequality that characterized the South. The auto industry's booming success enabled men of all colors to get assembly-line jobs, where they could make enough money to support their families. Grayson's father, who worked in quality control at the Ford Motor Company, took pride in supporting his five children. He could be angry at times—a leftover, his children felt, from his days of serving in a black platoon in the South Pacific during World War II—but he loved his family and he wanted his children to make something of their lives. Grayson, the second-oldest child in the family, was sure of a few things. One was that he didn't want to go to Vietnam, where his older brother was serving as a Marine. The second was that he wanted to go to college and play basketball.

Grayson was sitting at home on the night of April 4 when the phone rang. He rushed to pick it up so that the noise wouldn't wake his mother, who was resting before starting her night shift as a nurse. One of Grayson's teammates was on the other end of the line.

"Turn on the TV," he said to Grayson.

"What's going on?"

"Just turn on the TV. King has just been killed."

Grayson hung up without saying goodbye and ran to the TV set. There were images of dazed people milling around the hospital in Memphis, Tennessee, where King had been pronounced dead. President Lyndon B. Johnson had given a televised statement from the White House talking about the sadness he felt at the "brutal slaying" and asked "every citizen to reject the blind violence that has struck Dr. King." It was clear from the president's voice that he was worried about the possibility of riots, which were already starting to break out across the country. As he watched the screen, Grayson's confident excitement about the future was gone. In its place a cloud now seemed to hover above the country. He wondered whether Detroit was going to be destroyed again.

The city hadn't yet fully recovered from the chaos of the previous summer, when five days of looting, burning, and angry marches had left more than two thousand buildings destroyed, hundreds injured, and forty-three people dead. Grayson vividly recalled witnessing his neighbors' anger against the humiliating police tactics, and now he listened for the sounds of glass being smashed and people yelling. Yet Detroit seemed oddly quiet. Even so, his instinct was to stick close to home.

Everyone feared a repeat of 1967. Later he found out that there were some signs of protest elsewhere in the city, but nothing on par with what was happening in some other major cities. After the events of the previous summer, the Detroit police had learned how to clamp down quickly on troublemakers. That was fine by Grayson. The last thing he wanted to do was set buildings on fire to mourn the life of a man who preached nonviolence. It felt wrong, and he had his own future to worry about.

Years later, the investment banker and former deputy mayor of New York would still shake his head in sadness when thinking about King's death. "For me and my peers, it turned our worlds upside down," he said during an interview at the headquarters of M.R. Beal in lower Manhattan. "Here's a man who had asked people to judge him by the content of his character and not by the color of his skin. He had the power to make people act. You have to understand how much hope a lot of us had invested in Dr. King. When he died, I think a lot of that hope died with him."

Theodore V. Wells, Jr., had never seen anything like the tanks that were rolling through his neighborhood in Washington, D.C. He sat on the front steps of his small rowhouse with a friend, his eyes fixed on a parade of armored personnel carriers and army trucks that were all headed downtown to quell the riots. Wells noticed that troops from the Maryland National Guard were already stationed around the corner to prevent the arson and looting from spreading to his working-class neighborhood; tanks had even parked on the Coolidge High School football fields. A little more than a day had passed since King's death, but the area around Fourteenth Street had already been largely destroyed.

Wells's football coach was angry about the military presence. Although he understood the magnitude of the event and the seriousness of the violence that had broken out in response to it, being black himself he could hardly welcome the armed and mainly white soldiers who were stopping his team from practicing. Wells, though, felt both exhilarated and scared. As he passed through the school parking lot, he noticed a man standing beside the open trunk of his car, trying to sell clothes that had been stolen in the riot.

Theodore Wells

On the night of King's death, Wells and his friends had been playing pickup basketball on a court near the high school when his mother had come to tell him the news. Phyllis Wells was a mailroom clerk at the Department of the Navy, earning just enough to raise her son and his younger sister. Ma Wells, as she liked to be called, showered her children with love, and she did the same for the young friends and neighbors who constantly dropped by their home in northwest Washington. A good life, she told her children, was about putting in the effort. Having moved at eighteen from a small farm in Virginia to take a government job, she knew that success never came from laziness. But she also understood the power of laughter, community, and good food, and cooked a massive meal every Sunday for Ted and his friends. They, and everyone else in the neighborhood, adored Ma Wells.

As soon as she heard about King's death, Ma Wells immediately began to worry for her son. Ted—or "Tokey," as everyone in the neighborhood called him—was a diligent student and a star center on the school's football team. Out on the street, though, where rage was escalating fast, a six-foot-two, 230-pound black man could easily become a police target. Wells's mother went straight to the basketball court and insisted that her son and his friends come back to the house. They all followed her, unsure of what to do next.

The riots started slowly that night. Stokely Carmichael, a former chairman of the Student Nonviolent Coordinating Committee (SNCC) who had months earlier become prime minister of the Black Panther Party, held a press conference in the U.S. Capitol, calling the murder of Dr. King a declaration of war against black people. Carmichael then led mourners through the neighborhoods near Wells's home, asking that owners close their stores out of respect for King. The requests then turned to demands, and things escalated from there. Soon it hardly mattered what the store owners did: Some people just felt like lashing out. Carmichael was said to have told people to stay calm, but it was too late. Emotions were running high as hymns played from transistor radios, and TV networks ran clips of King's speeches. It didn't take long for the looting to begin.

Although the city was still calm enough on Friday morning for Wells and his sister, who was eleven years younger, to go to school, the situation deteriorated fast. By noon so many rioters were throwing rocks and bottles at cars that his mother couldn't get a ride home from work. Ted picked up his sister from school; when they got home, they could see the tanks and army trucks from their front porch. Ted had a passion for civil rights that had been nourished by living in the center of black Washington and attending occasional protest rallies. While he admired Carmichael and his calls for black power, he had no particular desire to rage against the establishment.

Wells was a good student, used to getting straight A's on his report cards and praise for his work ethic. Even in elementary school, he had kept track of his grades, creating his own report card long before the official one arrived. Once, when a teacher dared to give him a lower-than-expected mark, he went to her with his own handwritten record of his achievements and convinced her to raise the grade. He wasn't a protester by nature; he was a charmer, a leader, the one who stood up for classmates against bullies and could always make his teammates laugh. He had his sights set on Howard University, a historically black institution that had been Carmichael's alma mater and that was where President Johnson had delivered a landmark speech on civil rights a few years earlier. Howard was the kind of place where Wells could imagine himself becoming a leader.

By Sunday morning, more than eight hundred fires were burning across D.C., mostly in black neighborhoods. More than a thousand people were hurt, and twelve were dead, though Mayor-Commissioner Walter Washington had instructed the police not to shoot at rioters. The devastation was staggering: Hundreds of buildings had been reduced to rubble, wiping out the largely black-owned businesses in the area and destroying the livelihoods of the people who worked for them. In some cases, the scars would turn out to be permanent. Wells, at the age of seventeen, suddenly felt that his hometown would never be the same.

They were five young men at a pivotal point in their lives, but they were also coming of age at a time when their country was in a state of upheaval. Nineteen sixty-eight would turn out to be one of the most dramatic and difficult years in American history. January had brought the Tet Offensive, a series of surprise attacks by North Vietnamese troops that stunned the U.S. public and the military, raising doubts about the promise that victory was in sight. Within weeks, newscaster Walter Cronkite, "the most trusted man in America," had turned against the Vietnam War and concluded that the only way out of the stalemate was to negotiate for peace. As more members of the massive baby boom generation became eligible for military service, the resistance and anger at being forced to fight in the jungles of Southeast Asia increased. For many black Americans, Vietnam had become a civil rights issue. According to figures cited by King, who had come out against the war in 1967, the United States had spent $322,000 for each enemy killed in Vietnam and only $53 on each person it had classified as poor in its war on poverty. When former heavyweight boxing champion Muhammad Ali was asked shortly after King's death about the prospects of going to jail for resisting the draft, he told sportscaster Bud Collins that "blacks have actually been in jail for the 400 years we've been here in America." The war had become another source of racial tension due to the widespread perception that a disproportionate number of combat troops were black, in part because they lacked the resources to go to college and defer being drafted.

As Thomas, Wells, and the other men struggled to come to terms with King's death, they were unaware of the impact it was already starting to have on the college landscape. The assassination of the country's greatest civil rights champion had inspired many to turn their talk about equality into action. College administrators examined their curriculum, their faculty, and their policies to see how they might find a way to carry on the work of Dr. King. Many looked around their campuses and realized how little they had done to chip away at social inequality. For some, the sea of white faces that they had long taken for granted now became a source of shame. For Stan Grayson, some of the hope and promise of civil rights may have diminished with King's death. But for one man, Father John Brooks, the sudden sense of urgency gave him the resources and the authority to truly put the preacher's teachings into practice.

TWO

Against the Clock

John Brooks felt a sense of urgency as the white 1965 Pontiac GTO raced down the highway in April 1968. The forty-four-year-old priest was on a mission and he didn't have much time to complete it. After months of lobbying and debating, Brooks had been authorized to seek out black recruits and offer them full scholarships to the College of the Holy Cross. The question was whether he could find the right young men and, once he did, if he could convince them that Holy Cross was their best option. The best of the students, he suspected, would already have other plans. He had been talking to guidance counselors and potential recruits for months, and the school year was almost over.

His companion, Jim Gallagher, an admissions officer at Holy Cross, drove solemnly, his eyes fixed firmly on the road. At twenty-five, the clean-cut Gallagher was usually chatty and quick with a joke, but today he was overwhelmed with sadness.

Brooks tried to keep the conversation light, refusing to dwell on his own grief. Only a few days had passed since King had been rushed to the hospital in Memphis after being shot on the second-floor balcony of the Lorraine Motel, a nondescript place where King had stayed because it was owned by a black businessman. An hour later, at 7:05 P.M., King was pronounced dead.

As the anger and riots began to escalate across the country, Brooks sat alone in his room at the Jesuit residence and prayed. Years later he couldn't recall what first went through his mind the moment he heard that King had died, but he would always remember his resolution. He realized that simply grieving the loss of a great man of God wasn't going to amount to much; it was almost self-indulgent in light of the risks that King had taken to make the world a more just place. Brooks had

The Reverend
John Brooks

to stop talking about the need to bring more black students to Holy Cross and just make it happen. The desire hadn't started with King's death, nor was Brooks alone in pushing for it to happen, but things had stalled. Brooks had the ear and respect of many colleagues in the administration, but there was only so much that a theology professor could do. There were concerns about money and, specifically, how little of it the college could spare with its slim financial cushion. There were issues of fairness, as many of the trustees argued that black students were welcome to come if they cleared the same hurdles and were admitted through the same procedures as everyone else. The worst thing, they had warned, would be to foster the perception that one group was getting special attention over another. A sudden influx of black students might not sit well with the alumni, whose donations and loyalty to the college were based at least in part on the notion that it was going to prepare generations of their own children for success in the world.

Brooks had spent months talking with students, black and white, about what could be done. He had met with African American leaders and other academics in Worcester. He participated in lively debates within the Jesuit community, which had a long-standing mission of social justice and academic excellence, and now had to grapple with how to strike the right balance in its recruitment efforts at Holy Cross. If there was ever a time to heed King's call to action and take up the mantle of civil rights, it was in the wake of his death. Brooks sensed that the shock and outpouring of grief had finally created an opportunity to get a real commitment from the school, and he intended to make the most of it.

Brooks was just five years older than King, although his black-rimmed glasses, clerical collar, and graying hair made him look like he belonged to another era. The priest shared King's passion about the promise of social justice, especially following the bloody civil rights clashes in Selma, Alabama, three years earlier. He had been a newcomer to the Holy Cross faculty at that point, having just come back from an intoxicating stint in Rome. Where Clarence Thomas saw hypocrisy in the Roman Catholic Church's efforts to reevaluate and renew its role in the world, John Brooks saw hope. While living in Rome, he had immersed himself in the intense politics and drama of Vatican II. Between classes and study, he and his friends could be found hanging around the steps of the Vatican, getting updates on the latest missives and battles. Armed with a doctorate in theology from the Pontifical Gregorian University in Rome, Brooks arrived at Holy Cross convinced that a revitalized Church could become a leader in promoting social change. The Church had taken that role in the past and, Brooks believed, it could help make civil rights a reality. When he took his position at the college, he quietly vowed to help push Holy Cross toward enrolling more "Afro-Americans."

Even among the Jesuits, a progressive, intellectual, and typically outspoken order of the Church, John Brooks stood out. While many of the professors and priests at Holy Cross welcomed change, few were as relentless as Brooks in pushing for it. Some students who had taken his theology classes would later recall his preference for using the Bible as a jumping-off point to discuss current affairs, from the morality of the war to the messages in popular movies like *The Graduate* or *In the Heat of the Night*. While Brooks made it clear that nobody should show up to class unprepared, the professor was clearly less bothered by a student who didn't understand a topic than by one who didn't try to challenge himself in thinking about it. Some found it hard to tell at times whether Brooks was left-wing or conservative, as he could persuasively articulate both sides of an argument. When asked where on the political spectrum he might put himself, Brooks laughed and said he liked any side that supports individual thought. More important, he seemed to empathize with what drove different views. In an era of black and white, Brooks was unafraid to embrace views that were gray.

His stance on civil rights wasn't just moral but practical: There was an ambitious generation of black men growing up in America, and the college was missing out on a chance to help shape it. Holy Cross risked becoming less relevant by admitting so few black students. No college could pride itself on developing the nation's future leaders when it largely ignored the potential of an entire group of talented young men, and most of those men would probably never think of attending Holy Cross unless people like him made the effort to recruit them.

With King's assassination, the fight became more personal for Brooks. He looked around the campus and realized how little had been accomplished. Wooing black college recruits to Worcester was no easy task: There was little to recommend in the struggling industrial city, and Brooks knew the obvious challenges in attracting black men to a campus where practically all of the 2,200 students were white. Even though the college's first valedictorian had been the son of a slave, the campus had built its reputation largely on educating sons of the Irish elite. That's certainly how Brooks had come to study there. The darkest people Brooks had ever recalled seeing—both as a student and growing up near Boston's Fenway Park—were Italian or Portuguese. When it came to black students, there seemed to be an unspoken pattern emerging each year: One was admitted from the North, one from the South; one of those two would typically be on athletic scholarship, one on academic scholarship. The college rarely admitted more than two black men in any given year. When Brooks arrived to teach in the mid-1960s, a quiet Bostonian named Bob Credle was the only black student on the entire campus. For some in the administration, that was sufficient.

Even as the civil rights movement was growing in popularity on campus, Brooks knew there was resistance to change. He was pushing both the admissions and athletics departments to join in his effort to recruit black students. The biggest issue was scholarships. Every time Brooks asked about getting money, he was told it wasn't there. He suspected that the problem was less the school's paltry endowment than the fear that it could become even smaller if alumni caught wind of a black recruitment drive that might diminish the number of spots for their sons. Some faculty members claimed that it was unfair to bring "Negroes" to a place where they might not be equipped to succeed. Others privately questioned why Brooks, a professor who headed up the theology department, was making it his job to recruit students. But few faculty members openly criticized him. Brooks had a sharp wit and a short fuse, and there wasn't always much satisfaction in engaging him in debate. He would listen. He would understand. But his colleagues quickly realized that once Brooks made up his mind, he didn't have much interest in changing it. Understanding the complexities of different views rarely seemed to diminish his conviction in holding to his own. Despite his good-natured jokes and easy charm, which had made him a favorite with students, and his political savvy, which was useful in maintaining the warm relations he enjoyed with the president, he was a man who seemed almost oblivious to pressure from his peers. That quality in itself had become an irritant to some.

In the fall of 1967, several months before King's death, Brooks had asked Gallagher to join him on a trip to Philadelphia to visit Catholic high schools. They talked to guidance counselors at each school, who often seemed more perplexed than excited over the college's interest in African Americans. Ultimately the trip proved fruitless. Although Brooks met several promising candidates, he wasn't sure he could offer the students full scholarships. King's death made Brooks's case to the Holy Cross administration more compelling. Shortly after the assassination, Brooks went to the president of Holy Cross, Reverend Raymond J. Swords, to appeal for a fresh chance to interview black students and for the authorization to offer them admission and scholarships, bypassing the lengthy admissions process since it was too late in the school year to go through the usual channels. It was a daring move. Brooks pledged that anyone he picked would meet the faculty's standards and would have the right character for the college. In return he wanted the president to allow him to make decisions on the spot. Surprisingly, Swords agreed.

As Brooks and Gallagher drove to Philadelphia that spring, riots were breaking out across the country, leaving a landscape of shattered glass and flames. Back on campus, there was a quiet numbness and sense of disbelief. Many of the faculty and students at Holy Cross felt a connection to King, who had come to speak at the school five years earlier, in November 1962. King's photo had appeared in the yearbook that year, with a caption praising him for his "courage, conviction and eloquence."

Before leaving for Philadelphia, Brooks had hastily set up as many meetings as he could. He had decided to focus on Catholic high schools because he figured he could find young men there who were used to having both a rigorous academic schedule and some element of religion in their education. Although Brooks had yet to see many signs that other colleges were vigorously recruiting black students, he was sure it would start happening soon, and wanted to get to the kids first. He knew why Holy Cross was special, but the high school students might not, so he'd have to convince them. Visiting the Catholic high schools himself would give him an edge. There was already a pipeline and a reputation for Holy Cross in those schools, and they weren't a traditional hunting ground for the Ivy League colleges.

Brooks was also worried about Gallagher. At Brooks's request, the young recruiter had gone to an inner-city Chicago neighborhood to look for potential recruits. The news of King's assassination had left the admissions officer so traumatized that some of his colleagues were worried he might have a breakdown. The truth was, Gallagher had never planned on taking the recruitment job so much to heart; he was only taking a break after college to make some money before heading off to graduate school. But King's death had shaken him. Gallagher was feeling bereft and was relieved when Brooks called him back to Worcester to join him for a road trip to Philadelphia in mid-April.

It was still morning when both men drove past a building in the early stages of construction. St. Joseph's Preparatory School in Philadelphia, known as "the Prep," was a 115-year-old Jesuit high school that had burned down in 1966. The two men pulled up in front of the temporary quarters where classes were being held until the main building was restored. The city's streets were filled with people sporting Afros and long hair as they walked about in gauzy shirts, jeans, and sandals, but that wasn't the culture of the Prep, where students with short-cropped hair and blazers were making their way through crowded halls.

Both men were welcomed heartily by counselors at The Prep. It was rare to get a high-level visit from one of the country's most prestigious Catholic colleges, and each school was eager to show off its academic stars. Gallagher noticed that several members of the administration seemed a little miffed when Brooks made it clear that they were there to meet promising black students only. To save time, the two men decided to split up to do initial interviews. Brooks met with Gilbert Hardy, an accomplished sprinter and National Greek Scholar who was introduced to him as one of the brightest minds at St. Joseph's. Hardy struck Brooks as personable and thoughtful, a young man who was willing to work for what he wanted. Hardy talked about school, his family, and his ambitions, which were leaning toward law; Brooks explained the kind of preparation he could expect to get at Holy Cross, as well as the kind of support. By the end of their meeting, Hardy seemed enthusiastic about Holy Cross.

One at a time. That's how Brooks found them. He and Gallagher went to a handful of Catholic schools, interviewing dozens of candidates. They talked to teachers and counselors. At the end of the frenzied visit, the two men sat down together in a Philadelphia restaurant with a list of names. Together they picked out several young men who seemed to have what it would take to succeed at Holy Cross. For Brooks, the men's grades were just a starting point. The priest was equally interested in the candidates' drive and ambition. It would take a strong personality to overcome the isolation many would feel at Holy Cross. It was hard enough for the young men to attend white Catholic high schools when at least they would return to the comfort of their families and neighborhood friends at the end of the day. At Holy Cross, the isolation of the classroom would follow them to where they ate and slept. The curriculum would be tough, and the expectations high.

It wasn't just a matter of figuring out who could stick it out for four years. Brooks figured that many of them could do that. He wanted to find out which students would be trying to accomplish something more. The generation was ripe for producing leaders: They would have more rights and more opportunities than any group of black American men that had come before them. But they would also be tested in ways that their fathers and grandfathers hadn't been; they were being handed a chance to fail without necessarily being given all the support they needed to succeed, being shown the door to a room where they might not ultimately be welcome. A good education wouldn't erase the barriers or the prejudice, but Brooks knew it could be a powerful tool.

Brooks and Gallagher spent hours debating about the different candidates they had met—the ones who had the drive but not the grades, the ones who seemed bright but undisciplined, the ones who were tough and loud, and the ones who tried to stay hidden in the background. Brooks was a fast judge of character, but he considered himself to be a good one, too. Gallagher marveled at how much the priest had gleaned from such short meetings.

In the end, they found nine recruits from Philadelphia: Walter Roy, a determined-looking young man whose mother had recently died and who had told the priest that he was planning a career in politics; Harvey Wigfall, who'd made an impression on Brooks with his strong convictions about social justice; Gordon Davis, who'd said that he would have preferred to enter the army but was willing to come to Holy Cross because his father, a career soldier, had talked him into taking a deferment; Gil Hardy, the National Greek Scholar; Juan Brunzello, who planned to major in math; Craig Lewis, a flute player who decided to turn down Swarthmore to come to Holy Cross; Robert Stephens, another accomplished musician; Stephen Collins, a high school basketball star; and James P. Wynn, the valedictorian of his class at West Catholic Boys High School who wanted to study psychology.

Brooks committed more than eighty thousand dollars of the college's money to cover tuition, books, and residence for the nine recruits from Philadelphia for their four years at Holy Cross. He hadn't cleared the figure with President Swords, but he felt he could deal with any fallout from that later.

President Lyndon B. Johnson had responded to the national anguish over King's death by signing the Civil Rights Act of 1968 on April 11, and Brooks believed it could be the beginning of a fairer world. Brooks would keep pushing colleagues and students to understand the role they could play in helping to fulfill King's dream by bringing more black students onto campus and by helping them to flourish. On the night of April 4, King had told the Memphis crowd, "I'm happy tonight." Even with threats on all sides, the Baptist minister could see that people were pulling together to stand up for their rights. King knew that things weren't good, but he believed that they could get better. Sitting in a Philadelphia diner, looking at the names of the men who would now get a chance to pursue a college education, Brooks felt a moment of happiness, too. He hoped that some good could come of King's death.

THREE

First Impressions

The morning Brooks returned from Philadelphia, he went to see President Swords. They both knew that abandoning the usual admissions protocol was bound to raise eyebrows on campus. But if there was still opposition to admitting more black men to Holy Cross, few were vocal about it after King's death. Brooks knew he had a rare opportunity to push through his agenda. Before he had left for Philadelphia, he had helped to organize a student and faculty drive to raise money for a new Martin Luther King, Jr., scholarship.

Brooks's personal crusade had made him a controversial figure among his fellow professors. He was hardly the only person on campus who cared about issues of equality and civil rights, yet he had been the one behind this sudden drive to admit black students. Some admired his devotion, seeing him as a larger-than-life figure with a big heart and an admirable ability to push hard for what he believed in. Others on the faculty thought Brooks could be stubborn and dismissive once he'd made up his mind. He certainly made sure that every residence floor monitor was approached about helping to raise money for the cause, and that every professor got a letter asking him to solicit funds for the scholarship. His popularity with many of the students on campus helped—he had a remarkable facility for remembering their names as he stopped to chat with them between classes—but they raised barely enough money to support a handful of students. Still, Brooks felt the outreach had been an important gesture, even if it proved more valuable as moral support than as a source of funds. He also knew it might mollify alumni and colleagues who didn't want resources siphoned away.

Brooks would forever recall how uncharacteristically sheepish he felt as he walked into Swords's office to give him a report of his trip. The school's finances were hardly robust, and it was hard to argue that offering so many scholarships was fiscally responsible. He immediately blurted out to Swords that he had spent eighty thousand dollars of the schools' money. For a moment Swords said nothing. Then the president responded that he hoped it would be money well spent and quickly went back to his work. The onus was now on Brooks to prove that his gamble would pay off.

Brooks was grateful for his colleague's support, however stoic it might be. He knew that several alumni had already told Swords that they wouldn't take kindly to a special recruitment drive for black students. But Swords had become used to controversy during his eight-year tenure as president. Since taking the position in 1960, he had replaced a number of his fellow Jesuits with so-called lay faculty. His goal had been to improve the quality of teaching by tapping a wider and more diverse academic pool to fill tenured positions. The task had been a painful one, made more awkward by the fact that the priests shared a common residence. Every time Swords removed one of the brothers from an academic post, he knew he'd have to face that man every day in the dining room or the lounge of their shared home. Spending thousands of dollars on a drive to bring in black freshmen was just another one of the difficult choices he had to make.

Swords, a cerebral and sometimes aloof academic, had come to the president's job reluctantly. Although he had little desire to be in the public spotlight, he wasn't afraid to break with tradition when he felt it was necessary. Swords had done his best to raise the school's academic standards, for example, going outside the Jesuit community to hire professors with strong research and teaching credentials. He was a quiet man, often seen walking around campus with a set of rosary beads in his hands. His instinct was to share power, not hoard it, and Brooks had become, in many ways, his right-hand man. Brooks clearly had a greater appetite for conflict and dramatic change than Swords. Along with pushing to admit black men, Brooks had vigorously argued for the need to admit women, a move so radical that the school's trustees hadn't given it too much consideration in 1968. Brooks was so tenacious that even some of his sympathizers warned him that he risked sabotaging his own causes. Where others might work to persuade opponents, Brooks had an uncomfortable tendency to simply announce what needed to be done. He didn't feel he had time to worry about what others were thinking.

Barely a week after their Philadelphia trip, Brooks tapped Gallagher yet again, this time to help bring some of the men they had interviewed in the city up to Worcester for Spring Weekend. Brooks knew whom he wanted, and the recruits had confirmed their interest in attending Holy Cross, but there was still time for them to change their minds or be recruited to other schools. Acceptances would have started arriving in the mail; scholarship offers would be forthcoming and likely enhanced in the wake of King's assassination. The only way to make the men fully appreciate what Holy Cross could offer, Brooks believed, was to invite them to the campus to look around. A few might be willing to come with friends or parents, but he knew that many of the young men didn't have the money to make their way to Worcester on their own. The best thing would be to pick them up and bring them back himself.

Spring Weekend was the highlight of the Holy Cross year, with a headliner concert, Junior Prom, and a campus that would be in full bloom. It was a chance to show off Holy Cross at its best. For those recruits who were firmly committed to Holy Cross, Brooks believed that showing them the campus might reassure them. For those who might be quietly wavering, Spring Weekend might win them over.

Brooks asked the admissions office to see which of the men were interested in a free ride and weekend on campus. About half a dozen said yes. He inquired about other black students who might have an interest in Holy Cross. There was one young man in Washington, Ed

Jones, who had been referred to the college by a Jesuit priest. Brooks hadn't met Jones himself but the D.C.-based Jesuit had spoken highly of the teen's work ethic and intelligence. If they could arrange for a way to get Jones to Philadelphia, Brooks said, they could bring him as part of the larger group. With so many men to transport, they would need more than Gallagher's car, so Brooks borrowed an old station wagon from a colleague on campus. On the day they had agreed to meet, Brooks and Gallagher left early, arriving in central Philadelphia at the agreed-upon pickup spot before midday.

Back in Washington, Ed Jones left his home early to catch a bus to Philadelphia, where he would meet up with the priest who had offered to drive him to Worcester. The notion of a "spring" weekend was so foreign to him that it felt almost quaint, yet the idea that he was being invited as a guest of the college was hard to resist. No other school was courting him. Jones couldn't help wondering why Holy Cross was bothering to go to such an effort.

By the time Jones got to the pickup point in Philadelphia, a group of black teens was already milling around a broad middle-aged man with a clerical collar and another white man who didn't look all that much older than the students. The priest introduced himself as John Brooks.

Jones climbed into the backseat with teens Gordon Davis and Harvey Wigfall. As they drove off, he settled in to listen to the conversation. The men were discussing the recent social upheaval. On the outer edge of Harlem in New York, students at Columbia University were embroiled in what would turn out to be a dramatic and violent protest. Their main grievance, along with Columbia's ties to companies profiting from the war, was the university's treatment of residents in the surrounding neighborhood, many of whom were black. In particular, the protesters had targeted a ten-story gymnasium under construction in nearby Morningside Park that they said offered limited—and segregated—access to locals while taking up precious public space. In reaction, they had taken over campus buildings and held the dean hostage in his office. News of the takeover, which ultimately ended in a bloody clash with police and the suspension of classes, was playing on the radio as the Holy Cross recruits traveled north to get their own taste of college life. Cities were no longer burning, but the country was still on edge. Shortly after King's death, on April 7, Eldridge Cleaver had been wounded and a black teen was killed in a shootout with Oakland police. Jones admired Cleaver, in part because of his provocative statements as a spokesman for the Black Panther Party, a revolutionary group that had formed two years earlier in California to give blacks more power and control in their communities, especially against the actions of white police. More important, Cleaver had just released his searing *Soul on Ice*, a collection of essays he'd written in prison. *The New York Times* had praised it as a book about "the imprisonment of men's souls by society." That Cleaver had been shot and arrested so soon after the book's release somehow validated its message that the black experience was ultimately an anguished one. It felt like an odd time to be taking a field trip to a white Catholic college.

Jones liked to listen, and Brooks certainly liked to talk. He asked the young men what they thought of the Columbia students' demands. Jones could tell that the priest was the type who liked to keep people on their toes. Gallagher jumped into the conversation from time to time, but if the other young men had provocative views on what was going on—and Jones knew that he certainly did—few were eager to share them. Expressing sympathy with student radicals seemed like a sure route to getting a scholarship offer revoked.

Brooks told the men stories about the school while questioning them about other issues ranging from the war to bell-bottom pants. He clearly possessed a useful personality for winning over young minds. Although it didn't come naturally to him, Jones tried to engage in conversation with Davis. He felt he had no choice; the two of them were practically sitting on each other's laps. Davis had only just heard about Holy Cross the previous week. His plan had been to go to a state school until a guidance counselor at his high school had called him into the office to meet Brooks and Gallagher. Gordon didn't know much about Holy Cross, but he was interested in a weekend away from home and the prospect of a concert.

With the exception of a trip to Brooklyn in the summer of 1965, Jones hadn't spent any time in the North. To him it would always be the land of abolition. These were the descendants of the people who had fought to end slavery, whereas the white folks he saw while staying with his mother's family in Virginia were, he assumed, descendants of those who had fought to keep it. Jones was quietly impressed with Brooks and with the fact that he'd driven more than 250 miles from Massachusetts just to bring them up for a campus visit. None of the men in the wagon was a star athlete. There wouldn't be a dollar of revenue coming to the college when they enrolled. He wondered what Brooks saw in them.

The students reached Holy Cross as the sun was starting to set. The campus flowers were in bloom and the manicured grass had yet to endure the constant onslaught of Frisbee games and sunbathers that would arrive when the weather got warmer. But Jones and the other men were more interested in the students they saw wandering around the campus than in the landscaping. The students looked fresh-scrubbed and conservative with their short hair and sport jackets. Black or white, any of the students on campus would have stood out on the streets of Philadelphia and Washington, where the youth movement had inspired a much looser and more colorful look.

Stan Grayson had flown in from Detroit for the weekend. Holy Cross was one of several schools considering him for a basketball scholarship, and Jack Donohue, the Holy Cross basketball coach, had arranged for his trip. As Grayson walked across the field, he took in the beauty of the campus. It was undeniably pretty—a word he hadn't used all that often in his hometown, except perhaps to describe the girls in his neighborhood.

While Brooks was chatting with Jones, Donohue was eagerly wooing Grayson to come play for Holy Cross. The college had a solid team—they had won 15 of their 23 games the previous year—but they had a tendency to choke near the end of the season. Donohue saw great potential in Grayson. At six-foot-four and 205 pounds, Grayson would not be the biggest player on the court, but he was versatile and strong. And he was good at the tough stuff, like getting offensive rebounds and playing tenacious defense. Donohue knew that Grayson's skin color would be a bonus in securing the young man a scholarship, especially with Brooks's mission and mandate.

Although Grayson had been recruited by a number of schools, Holy Cross seemed to be the most eager to have him come. He wasn't sure why, since it hadn't really been a force in basketball since the 1940s, when George Kaftan, one of Brooks's best friends, and Bob Cousy had helped lead the team to an NCAA championship victory. But Donohue was trying to revive basketball at Holy Cross, and Grayson had come to believe that the college could offer him more than just an opportunity to hone his basketball skills. During a meeting with some alumni, one asked him what he wanted to do when he finished college. Grayson mentioned his interest in law. He didn't really see himself in a courtroom, but he knew that a career in basketball wouldn't last forever. Later, one of the interviewers sent him a list of law schools that the graduates of 1967 were currently attending. Nobody from any other school had sent a list of successful graduates. The alumnus who sent the list had also offered to help him pick the right classes to get into law school.

The more Grayson thought about it, the more he liked the idea of attending a school that boasted a reputation for academics as well as a decent team. In his view, a law degree would remove any doubts about ability and race. Lawyers didn't have to go begging for a chance to get through the doors of corporate America. They could make things happen. Basketball was going to be his ticket to college but Grayson didn't want to make it his only bet for getting ahead in the world.

Grayson found himself liking Coach Donohue, who had a wicked sense of humor and often joked that the Jesuits might have taken a vow of poverty, but he was being forced to live it. Donohue had come to Holy Cross from Manhattan's Power Memorial Academy, where he'd coached a much-buzzed-about player—Lew Alcindor, who later changed his name to Kareem Abdul-Jabbar. Donohue had sheltered Alcindor from the growing media frenzy and had helped him pick the University of California at Los Angeles for college.

Grayson toured the Holy Cross campus with a black sophomore named Art Martin as his guide. Martin had recently returned from representing the college at King's funeral in Atlanta. Grayson was enjoying the company of his chatty companion, unaware of Martin's reservations about having to show another black athlete around Holy Cross. Brooks had asked Martin to help with recruitment, and the sophomore felt an obligation to the priest. Martin hadn't told Brooks about the "Martin Luther Coon" jibe he'd heard on the night that King died, nor was he going to tell any potential recruit that they could find a much easier place to spend the next four years of their college life. Martin could tell that Grayson was an immensely likable man. The basketball player was walking around with a smile on his face, as if he already knew he would enjoy life at Holy Cross.

To Grayson, the campus felt miles away from the turmoil of Detroit. He would have a chance to work with the man who had coached Lew Alcindor in high school, and he would be getting a quality education that nobody could question. That said, he wasn't oblivious to the drawbacks of enrolling at Holy Cross: After four years of being the black guy at his high school, he wasn't eager to spend another four in a similar role at college. But he figured he could live with that. He made friends easily, black or white.

Martin was pleased that Grayson seemed so confident about Holy Cross. On a gut level, Martin desperately wanted more black men on campus. He was tired of classmates coming up to him any time they saw a black female to tell him they'd found a woman for him to date. There were so few black people living in Worcester—a little more than a thousand, by most counts—that there wasn't much relief in a night out in town. It would have been nice to have had a few more black peers to socialize with. He sometimes felt like the invisible man, accepted as part of the crowd because he wasn't radical or the kind of dangerous black man who might harbor ill will against whites. He was not, as one classmate had said that year in apparent admiration, "a nigger."

While he would have loved to have someone like Grayson for a friend, Martin also felt an obligation to make potential recruits like Grayson understand how tough Holy Cross could be. The only reason Martin had enrolled was that he was awarded a scholarship, and his parents couldn't afford to send five kids to college on a postal worker's wages. But Holy Cross wasn't always the tolerant and welcoming environment he had hoped it would be. For Martin, one event spoke volumes about the mind-set at Holy Cross. In February he had asked that the team boycott an annual track-and-field meet sponsored by the all-white New York Athletic Club. If the prestigious club wouldn't let someone with his skin color join its ranks, he told his coach, he didn't want to run in its event. Teams from other schools were dropping out of the meet for the same reason, as outrage mounted over the club's racist policies. But Holy Cross refused to drop out. While his coach told him that it would be fine for him to sit out the meet, the rest of the team showed up at Madison Square Garden. *The New York Times* even ran a photo of the Holy Cross bus arriving. Months later, Martin still felt sore that not one of his teammates had supported him.

There was no real sense of community among the eight black students already on campus, though Martin didn't really want to share that fact with the amiable recruit he was showing around. He was trying to help Father Brooks. In Martin's freshman year, the priest had been his religion class professor and had made a point of complimenting him on every track-and-field victory. Brooks was the one who'd found the money to fly him and another black student to Atlanta for King's funeral. While they didn't actually get inside the church where King's body lay, they had been inspired by the atmosphere. As Martin later wrote in *The Crusader,* the school newspaper, "I saw co-operation between white and black. I heard speakers encouraging the brotherhood of men. . . . The only way out is to work together." Though part of him had wanted to give Grayson a realistic view of campus life, Martin's overwhelming instinct was to encourage Grayson and the other black athletes who came his way. The reasons were personal: He hoped there could finally be a viable community of black students at the school.

Martin also found it heartening to see that Eddie Jenkins was back on campus for the weekend. He had met Jenkins earlier in the year when the high school football player was considering a number of different schools. While Jenkins had told Martin that Massachusetts had held no allure for him, his father had pressured him to visit both Boston College and Holy Cross. Jenkins immediately preferred Boston College. A friend of his had told him about the parties, the football, and the easy courses he could take at BC. But Jenkins had worked too hard in high school to settle for easy. When he visited Holy Cross a week later, the prop plane flying into Worcester made so many turns on the windy landing that Jenkins looked like he was about to throw up when he and Martin had met at the airport. And at the time Martin was feeling so bitter about the New York Athletic Club event that he hadn't been in a mood to sugar-coat his pitch to the potential recruit.

"You sure you want to do this, man?" Martin had said. "You go to a party around here and there's not a sister in the place." The only good thing about Holy Cross, he noted, was that it seemed to put people on a course to get into good law schools.

Jenkins had just laughed. If there was law school in his future, it would be years away. He couldn't see himself living with a bunch of white men in a frigid city where the planes couldn't land. Even the buildings looked miserable beneath mounds of snow. And Martin's words had hit home. Jenkins didn't see the point in attending a school where meeting a black woman at a party would feel like winning the lottery. Several other schools, including Florida A&M, were also interested in recruiting him. He saw no reason to choose Holy Cross over them.

After that winter visit, Martin had assumed he would never see Jenkins again. And yet here he was back on campus. Jenkins greeted Martin as if they were old friends. Although he still wasn't thrilled at the prospect of spending four years at Holy Cross, he was starting to see the sense in it. Part of the reason for his change of heart was the encouragement of Vincent O'Connor, his coach at St. Francis Prep. The high school was linked into the Catholic college network and was a popular stop for football recruiters. O'Connor had taken a liking to Jenkins and was trying to give his talented young player as much exposure as possible. He even brought Jenkins to big-name events like the Heisman Trophy dinner at the Downtown Athletic Club in Manhattan. It had been fun until a white club member told Jenkins to take a good look at the trophy because he would never see it again—the implication, Jenkins assumed, being that he would never be good enough to win it or white enough to be invited back. The comment had ruined his night.

O'Connor had also invited Jenkins and his father to another private club in Manhattan, this time to meet with some alumni from Boston College and Holy Cross. The coach had enough experience navigating the scholarship process for young players to know that it was the parents who were critical to reach. That seemed especially true for Jenkins, a teen with remarkable athletic talent who had still managed to maintain a strong B-plus average. On his own, Jenkins might not have seen much sense in sacrificing the big-time football experience to get a top-notch education, but Jenkins's father was seeking more than just a great sports program for his son. Having struggled to support the family by delivering papers, pumping gas, and doing odd construction jobs until he was hired by the post office, Jenkins's father understood the value of an education. As they walked to where the small alumni group had gathered, Jenkins tried to hide his discomfort at seeing white men in sport coats and stiff collars, holding tumblers of alcohol in one hand and cigars in the other. O'Connell had told him that some of the men were lieutenants of J. Edgar Hoover, then director of the Federal Bureau of Investigation, and he was immediately convinced that they were all spies. After some jovial banter about the merits of Boston College versus Holy Cross, one of the men asked Jenkins about his career ambitions beyond football. Jenkins immediately blurted out that his dream was to get a law degree, though he decided to leave out his utter lack of interest in the FBI.

Jenkins wasn't sure who at Holy Cross was primarily responsible for the interest in him, but it was clear that he had caught someone's attention. It was true that during one game in his senior year of high school, Jenkins had met Dennis Golden, the Holy Cross freshman football coach, who then convinced him to fly to Worcester for what turned out to be a disheartening midwinter visit, and Jenkins had also met head coach Tom Boisture, who was interested in Jenkins as a wide receiver and who had somehow convinced him to come back for Spring Weekend. But Jenkins sensed there was something more than a coach's interest going on behind the scenes, a motivation that started to become clear when he was greeted and shown around by one of the only black students on campus. This was a college, he realized, that was desperate to get some brothers on campus. Jenkins wasn't bothered by that. In fact, he found it heartening that the people running Holy Cross might feel as uncomfortable with its overwhelming whiteness as he did.

Jenkins could at least see that Holy Cross looked much better in the spring. To start with, there were a lot of women milling around, although few were black and he assumed that the energy of Spring Weekend wasn't an indication of everyday life on campus. Even so, he was warming to the place, especially now that he could speak without his breath forming clouds in the air.

Eddie headed to the top of Mount St. James, as they called the hill where team practices took place, and immediately noticed Ted Wells. They both looked relieved to see a fellow brother on the field and struck up a conversation. Jenkins was impressed by the fact that Wells played center on his high school team; it was a position that required someone to snap the ball to the quarterback and direct the offensive line, a job that could only be done well by someone who understood the playbook and could quickly read the defense's strategy to make the right call. Wells, meanwhile, immediately liked Jenkins's sense of humor and easygoing confidence. Eddie Jenkins came across as a man who assumed the world was full of friendships waiting to be formed. The two quickly found themselves laughing and joking with each other. Having Jenkins around would make attending Holy Cross a lot easier, Wells thought.

In truth, Wells was only partly interested in the school's football team. Blocking and tackling weren't going to be his life; they were a means to an end. He didn't want to go to a big football school where he might be stereotyped as a dumb jock. And Wells wasn't really looking to meet women. He was still dating his high school girlfriend, though that didn't look so promising now that she was moving to Cincinnati in the fall to attend the College of Mount St. Joseph.

The scholarship offers had started arriving when Wells was a junior in high school: first a pitch from Morgan State, a black college in Baltimore, then offers from Hampton Institute (later Hampton University) and North Carolina A&T State University. The white universities began soliciting Wells during his senior year. When the University of Pittsburgh offered him a football scholarship, it had seemed too good to pass up. Wells agreed to enroll, and the story was covered in the local newspapers. Still, the offers kept coming. Haverford College offered to pay room, board, and tuition for four years. Penn State invited him down for a trial on its team.

Then Boisture had come to see Wells. The Holy Cross coach was able to put together an attractive offer, bolstered by the knowledge that the administration would fully support any effort to recruit black athletes. Even so, Wells had turned the coach down. While academics were his main priority, if he was going to play football, he wanted to play for a team that had more name recognition. But Boisture's visit, along with the offers from other schools, had made him curious. No longer content to settle on Pittsburgh, Wells had started to consider other options. And being wooed by Holy Cross impressed his Catholic girlfriend, not to mention her father. So he had decided to give the college a serious look.

Until he met Jenkins on the football field, though, Wells felt unsure about Holy Cross. It felt a universe away from his world in Washington. Wells vaguely recalled meeting a few white children in kindergarten, right after the Supreme Court had voted in *Brown v. Board of Education* that segregation was unconstitutional. But by the time he had reached high school, almost all of the white families had left his neighborhood and practically everyone in his classes was black.

Wells found himself to be a little uncomfortable with the prospect of playing on a white team, but he liked Boisture. From what he could see, the low-key coach seemed to have a sixth sense about talent and a real handle on the game. Boisture was thirty-seven and had just been promoted to head coach the year before. Dennis Golden, a decade his junior, would be managing the freshman players. One issue was finding the right role for Wells on the team. His high school coach had recommended to Golden that they consider letting him continue as center. Golden and Boisture seemed skeptical that he could handle it. Penn State hadn't considered him for that role, either. When Wells's coach had asked the recruiters why, he was told that it required a sophisticated understanding of the game. Wells interpreted that to mean they thought the position was too difficult for a black man.

For Jenkins, the quality of the team was a much more important consideration than which position he would play. He was betting on football as a ticket to success, and he knew that a great team and a great coach were going to be critical if he was to have a shot at a professional career. He also wanted to earn a degree that could take him to criminal law; football, if he made it, wouldn't last forever. The incident that sealed Jenkins's decision to come to Worcester occurred during a tour of the campus. An assistant coach had been showing Wells and him around, pointing out the facilities and talking about the traditions of Holy Cross. Clearly eager to win over the two young athletes, the coach brought them to the top of Mount St. James, scanned the horizon, and said, "You Nigros, I think you're really going to like it here." Jenkins looked over at Wells, who responded with raised eyebrows. It wasn't the fact that he'd called them both Negroes. Although *black* had become the preferred term for Jenkins's generation, *Negro* was still acceptable enough that Walter Cronkite had even used it on air to describe King on the night of the assassination. But there was something about the way the assistant coach had said it, something about his unwitting mixture of condescension and ignorance that made Jenkins conclude that the revolution on the streets had yet to reach the campus of Holy Cross.

Jenkins was sensitive to such comments. Racial inequality had become a topic of open and contentious debate in New York City, playing out in battles over everything from how black children were being educated in Brooklyn to Columbia University's real estate ambitions on the edge of Harlem. Jenkins also had family connections to the South. His father had been born into a family of sharecroppers in Georgia, and had grown up largely with a great-aunt in Jacksonville, Florida. His mother was one of twenty-one children of a white Scottish father and a black mother. Eddie was the youngest of four children. In 1954 his father had piled the family in the car, leaving Jenkins's five-year-old brother behind to keep his grandparents company, and drove up to New York. By moving north, Jenkins's father had hoped to escape the sting of the South's Jim Crow laws, which had forced blacks to go to separate schools, restaurants, toilets, and even public spaces. For Jenkins, then four, the most memorable thing about that long ride was watching his parents anxiously drive past a series of gas stations with whites-only public toilets while his older sister kept telling them that she needed to use a bathroom. When they finally found a station that had a facility for "colored" customers, everyone in the car was ordered to use it. The whites-only facilities didn't seem to fade until they hit northern Virginia. Even as his parents left behind such visible signs of segregation and bigotry, their awareness of it remained. Nobody was going to treat their children as second-class citizens.

For Jenkins, the message had stuck. Holy Cross was a college that seemed eager—more eager than any other school, in fact—to bring him on board, and yet he felt talked down to. He was being called a "Nigro" in the same way that white teenagers might address an older black man as "boy," and the assistant coach hadn't even realized he had said anything offensive. Yet Jenkins felt less insulted than empowered. He suddenly sensed that he might be able to make a difference at Holy Cross. He could bring a dose of black reality to the brothers in Worcester.

Wells, too, had decided by the end of the weekend that he wanted to attend Holy Cross. He had looked into the economics program, the major he intended to pursue, and was impressed with the rigor of the program. But he had to go back home to unravel the mess he had created for himself. He had already signed a contract to play for the University of Pittsburgh, and he didn't know how to get out of it. Holy Cross asked alumnus and board member Edward Bennett Williams to help by looking into what could be done. Williams was part owner of the Washington Redskins football team and a high-powered lawyer who had represented Senator Joe McCarthy and jailed Teamsters boss Jimmy Hoffa. When Williams called Wells at home to tell him he had checked into the Pittsburgh deal and nothing would happen if Wells broke it, the teen had nothing to say. "So my advice," Williams added, "is that you go to Holy Cross." After hearing that Wells had signed with Holy Cross, Boston University's coach upgraded his offer of a half scholarship to a full one. But Wells had made up his mind. He had found a strong school, a talented coach, and the start of a promising friendship, not to mention an institution that could only enhance his image in the eyes of his girlfriend's father.

The decision was easy for Ed Jones. Nobody was calling him with rival offers. Boston College had already turned him down, but he hadn't made much of an effort there. In fact, he hadn't really applied anywhere else except to low-cost public colleges near his home. He had never been the type to pursue bold ambitions. Nobody had ever tried to push him. In many ways Jones felt he was being pulled by Holy Cross. The people he met there, especially Father Brooks, seemed to see more in him than he saw in himself. It was a foreign feeling, but he liked it: the feeling of being wanted.

Jones didn't know what to expect from a Jesuit college. He had attended a Catholic school briefly as a child, when he was five. His mother had heard it was a good place to learn. One of the nuns, seeing him outside the building one morning, dropped him off at a first-grade classroom, and when he managed to keep up, nobody thought to move him back to kindergarten. Within months, though, he was pulled out of the school. His mother couldn't afford to pay even the greatly reduced fees on wages that rarely amounted to more than a hundred dollars a month. Jones ended up in a public school, but he never forgot the experience. The nuns had been nice to him, and the classrooms were clean. Though he wasn't religious, it gave him a good feeling about a Catholic education.

Now his mother seemed pleased, even slightly intimidated, that her son was going to college, especially since she herself had never been able to read or write. As soon as Jones could spell, he had signed his mother's name on report cards. His mother had learned to keep her own dreams modest, since even the small ones had a habit of being broken. As Jones recalls, anytime he had tried to ask her a question, she would sigh and say: "Why you ask me for?" But when he told her about the offer from Holy Cross, and the fact that they didn't have to pay, she seemed quietly proud, as if marveling that her long years of hardship and despair had somehow left her eldest boy intact.

Clarence Thomas was preparing to leave Immaculate Conception Seminary in Missouri. In the week after King's death, he had joined a march to honor King's life. The sense of brotherhood he felt at the gathering, so missing from the atmosphere at school, had only strengthened his conviction to leave the seminary. Thomas didn't know what he would do next. He didn't have money, and he suspected that it was too late to get into a college for the fall. But his biggest fear was telling his grandfather that he had broken his promise to become a priest.

In May, Thomas returned to Savannah and told his grandfather, Myers Anderson, the news. While his grandfather's wife was sympathetic to Clarence, it didn't change matters. A day later his grandfather told him to leave. Anderson claimed to be upset that Clarence had stayed out late the night before, but Thomas knew the real reason his grandfather was upset: He had shamed the family. From cloistered preparation for the priesthood, Thomas was suddenly cast out on his own. It was, he recalls, one of the most anxious times of his life. Thomas went to stay with his mother and soon found a summer job proofreading the copy on paper bags at a factory in Savannah. Besides the janitor, he was the only black man there.

He had no intention of spending his life in a factory. A local college seemed like the only option, until a Franciscan nun who had taught him at St. Pius X High School suggested that he look into Holy Cross. She had given the same advice to several other promising black students, including Bob DeShay, a Holy Cross sophomore who had attended St. Pius with Thomas for nine years. While Thomas was too late to apply through regular channels, he might be allowed to transfer. Thomas may have hated his experience at the seminary, but that hadn't curbed his work ethic: His grades had been among the best in his class. When the nun reached out to DeShay, he agreed to give Thomas a call to try to convince him to come to Holy Cross, even though DeShay was far from being a big supporter of the college.

DeShay hadn't adjusted well to Holy Cross. Although he had entered the college with high grades, he had been "invited" to leave the chemistry program at the end of his first year. His preparation at St. Pius apparently hadn't brought him up to the speed of the Holy Cross program. He had transferred to economics, where he was deeply unhappy and struggling to hold a B-plus average.

But DeShay knew he couldn't blame the college for his grades. What angered him was the magic wand that had appeared for black recruits after King's death. Before that time, Brooks had asked him to help to spread the word about Holy Cross to black students. Brooks had also approached Art Martin and some of the other black students, though he didn't press the few who clearly had no interest in being part of a black community. He never asked them to paint a rosy picture of life at Holy Cross. If anything, it was the opposite. He said he wanted potential recruits to have a chance to ask the black students about the realities of college life and hear from them about the benefits of an education at Holy Cross.

DeShay had agreed, even though it had struck him as ironic that he was being asked to do volunteer work when the school had sent him a clear message that he wasn't performing up to academic standards. Still, DeShay understood the value of the education he was getting and had gone out to chat up some promising high school students. Although the effort seemed scattered and somewhat futile without a bold plan to back it all up, DeShay had done his bit to talk up the school. Once the purse strings suddenly loosened after King's death, however, nobody seemed interested in his help. And DeShay felt he had been played for a fool.

Now that he had a particular recruit in mind, though, DeShay could finally do some good. Hell, yeah, DeShay thought to himself, he could help Thomas get to Holy Cross. He got on the phone and convinced his old friend that if anyone was going to get an exception for a late application, it would be a former priest-in-training. And he was sure the money would be there.

Thomas grudgingly agreed to put his name forward. Transferring to another Catholic college might not have been his first choice, but he knew that Holy Cross had a strong academic record. He knew he could handle the workload, and he could put up with being in another white school if it opened doors to something else. He didn't have many other options. He was stuck in a tiny apartment with his mother, working at a company where every day he had to stare at the words *nigger* and *KKK* scrawled across the bathroom stall.

On the morning of June 5, as Thomas was getting ready to go to work, he turned on the radio to hear that Bobby Kennedy had been shot. As Thomas later wrote in his autobiography, he fell to his knees and cried. Another great man had been struck down in hatred, and Thomas knew that someone somewhere was rejoicing at the news. This time his grief turned to anger and fueled a determination to do something more with his life. As Thomas later put it, he didn't want to let the bile and despair build up; that would only make his life worse. When DeShay called again, Thomas listened intently.

Holy Cross accepted Thomas's last-minute application and offered him a full package of financial aid. At Brooks's request, Coach Tom Boisture called up Thomas's grandfather to help smooth things over. Brooks thought that Boisture, who knew the South and had attended Mississippi State in the 1950s, might be able to put Myers Anderson's mind at ease. Though it wasn't Boisture's style, he found it was hard to say no to Brooks, and he made the call. When Anderson came to the phone, he sounded impatient, but once he understood the nature of the call, he began to listen. Boisture talked about how tough the Holy Cross curriculum could be, and how good the school would be for Thomas. Anderson didn't ask many questions and Boisture didn't know if their conversation had made any difference. Boisture didn't know the depth of acrimony between Thomas and his family. He never learned if Thomas had asked for his grandfather's consent, or if the older man gave it. Boisture hung up with the distinct feeling that Anderson had no intention of letting his grandson know that the Holy Cross football coach had called.

The very fact that Holy Cross wanted him gave Thomas hope at a time when his future seemed to be closing in on him. Thomas didn't need anyone's consent or any second opinion to know what to do with the opportunity that had suddenly been handed to him. He wasn't going to waste it, and this time he wouldn't care about fitting in.

FOUR

Come Together

In the summer of 1968, John Brooks was named vice president for academic affairs and dean at Holy Cross. The power he had unofficially assumed while head of the theology department was now officially his. *The Crusader* kicked off the school year with a profile of their new dean. On paper there seemed to be little difference between Brooks's views and those held by people half his age. He talked about the failure of universities to get involved in social issues and spoke out against the Vietnam War, declaring the draft unfair because it put the biggest burden on the "poor and the oppressed members of society." He called for an "offensive against the racism" on campus, and he talked about the need for "healthy dissent" against the Catholic stance on subjects like birth control. His views were aggressive, if not radical, for someone in a key role at one of the leading Catholic universities in the country. While Brooks was always quick to temper his bluntness with an easygoing smile and wit, his colleagues would later recall a man who openly shared his students' discomfort with the status quo. Unlike those students, though, he also understood the fears of an older generation and appreciated the need to at least try to bring people on board. He didn't want Holy Cross to descend into the kind of acrimony and combativeness that was turning campuses elsewhere into educational battlefields. A college couldn't

Father Brooks at a protest in 1971 against the Air Force ROTC program

survive if it treated its students as the enemy, but neither could it thrive if everyone else was left on the other side of the fence.

Still, Brooks was part of the establishment and knew that no amount of sympathetic rhetoric would make his first year as dean an easy one. The incoming generation of students was a restless one, full of varying degrees of indignation about everything from rising troop levels in Vietnam to the treatment on the home front of women, blacks, gays, Native Americans, the poor, and anyone under the age of twenty-five. Some were angry for the sake of being angry; others felt a genuine pain at the inequality in society. And as part of the largest generation the country had ever seen, born amid the boom times following World War II, they had numbers on their side. The incoming class of 1972 may have chosen Holy Cross for the same reasons as their fathers and grandfathers before them, but Brooks could see that their ambitions extended far beyond finding a job with a decent salary upon graduation. Right now, at least, they wanted to tear down old structures and build a new society, and they didn't necessarily care if the rest of the world went along with them. Having already dealt with the occasional protest the year before, Brooks knew that outlook wasn't going to create a peaceful atmosphere. The best he could hope for was that he and like-minded colleagues could convince the rest of the administration to give the students some space and treat the inevitable protests as demonstrations of free speech instead of a threat to the college.

Because of Brooks's efforts, in the fall of 1968 black students now had a somewhat visible presence among the 2,200 students on campus. The new arrivals included nineteen freshmen and Thomas, a sophomore. There were the nine men from Philadelphia and the four athletes—Eddie Jenkins, Ted Wells, Stan Grayson, and a Washington football player named Jaffe Dickerson. The rest were an eclectic mix: Ed Jones; Alfred Bruce Coleman of Georgia; Worcester native Leonard Cooper; William Bryant of Hollis, Queens, New York; Jeff Graham of Schenectady, New York; and Robert Louis Robards of Fair Haven, New Jersey. Brooks had personally written up files on most of these students, highlighting what set them apart from other young men. For some it was a challenging family background that they had already shown signs of overcoming. For others Brooks noted a willingness to push beyond expectations and give back to their communities in big and small ways. Not all of them were obvious candidates. He had to push for Ed Jones to be admitted. The Washington native's marks were far from spectacular, but Brooks liked his quiet intensity. The young man's high school teachers had been impressed with his reasoning and discipline, especially given the hardship of his background. And Brooks had noticed that there was always a book in Jones's hands. To him, that said something.

Brooks knew the least about the four students arriving on athletic scholarships. What he did know—and Wells, Jenkins, and Dickerson did not—was that the football players were arriving at a time when the Holy Cross football program was under mounting pressure to perform. Although the college competed against big sports schools like Syracuse University and Penn State, it was barely able to keep up. And while other colleges were ramping up their sports programs, Holy Cross was cutting back on athletic scholarships, part of an overall cost-cutting drive. But many in the administration had also argued that it didn't make sense to keep competing against teams that had more money, more fanfare, and more victories. By the fall of 1968 there was talk of dropping football altogether. Even the student newspaper, *The Crusader,* was in favor of curtailing the football program, running an editorial calling on Holy Cross to "scale its athletic program to the size and the academic goals of the college." While the specter of cuts no doubt weighed on Holy Cross's coaching staff that year, they certainly hadn't mentioned it as part of their pitch to the new recruits, black or otherwise. But they had sold all of them on the idea that Holy Cross would offer them more than just football. However, the new recruits might also have been disturbed to learn that their reputation had taken a hit before they even showed up. A study commissioned in 1966 had found the average SAT scores of athletes on the Holy Cross campus to be about 10 percent lower than the scores of other students. For those who opposed the college giving out scholarships to recruit "dumb jocks," it was another fact to add to the argument.

After a large and raucous farewell party in New York, a bleary-eyed Jenkins had a friend drive him up to Worcester the next morning. The two of them got lost in the towns of central Massachusetts; in every neighborhood they drove through, the streets were so quiet that it was hard to even find people to get directions from. By the time they reached Holy Cross, Jenkins didn't feel the excitement he had hoped for. Even the second-largest city in the state felt like a ghost town compared to New York City. Back home in Queens, the streets would have been humming with music and laughter and the sounds of parents yelling from their windows to children hanging out on the sidewalks below, but Worcester seemed to lack energy. It didn't help that Jenkins was one of the first students to arrive on campus, since the football players had to show up earlier than other students for practice. Jenkins flashed back to his visit the previous winter, when clusters of pale young men trudged across campus in heavy coats. He'd thought his impression of the college would improve with the warmer weather, but now he had further doubts. He and his friend found their way to his residence hall, which was still empty except for his fellow football players. Jenkins walked into a bare double room and threw his bags on one side; his future roommate hadn't arrived yet. After covering one wall with album covers from jazz singer Nancy Wilson and a photo of a girlfriend in New York, he felt more at home.

When Jenkins got to practice, Wells was already on the field where the freshman recruits were gathering. Wells had spent the summer in Washington moving furniture to earn some cash and was still feeling good about his decision to enroll. The Holy Cross campus felt as foreign to him as it did to Jenkins, but Wells hadn't set his expectations high for the social side of college life. Holy Cross would be his ticket to an Ivy League degree of some sort later on, maybe a law degree or a Ph.D., or both. His job was to study hard in class and play hard on the field. He'd do what he had to do, then move on. The thing that nagged at him most was that he missed his girlfriend, Nina Mitchell. They had decided to end their relationship that summer because of geography. She was heading off to spend the next four years in Cincinnati while he would be studying in Worcester at a college he'd chosen, in part, to impress her father. High school romances were supposed to end when you headed to college. Besides, everywhere he turned, someone was preaching the merits of free love. But he couldn't stop thinking about her.

At practice Wells found himself warming instantly to Dennis Golden. Golden was a tough coach, but he seemed honest and straightforward in his approach. With his dark hair, prominent features, and massive hands, the young man reminded players of the butler, Lurch, from the TV series *The Addams Family.* His style of football was simple: Whoever could block the hardest, tackle the hardest, run the hardest, and make the fewest mistakes would win the game. He wasn't interested in any debates about X's and O's and formations. Wells, on the other hand, had enjoyed the mental challenges of football from his days of playing center in high school. He was used to having a say in how the game was played. From the first day of practice he felt comfortable enough with Golden to question him about different plays. Wells also enjoyed entertaining the other freshmen players with impromptu quips such as "stay on my hip, and don't give me no lip." It was his way to break the ice and keep the mood light. Not a practice would pass without Wells sprinkling in some witty rhymes and raps, to which Golden would jokingly respond by suggesting he shut up and play.

Jaffe Dickerson, the other Washington, D.C., athlete, was only about five-foot-eight but he was fast, having broken track records at his old school. He came from a middle-class Catholic family and spoke with a careful enunciation. When he was looking at colleges, Dickerson had fielded calls from Virginia, Maryland, and even California before his father had said yes to Holy Cross without even telling him. His father had decided it was the best place for his son to get an education. Dickerson hadn't found out until it was too late to go anywhere else. He, too, wasn't

excited to have landed in Worcester, yet he understood the merits of getting a free education at a well-regarded college. Dickerson had no illu-
sions about carving out a long-term career in football.

There was a fourth black football recruit, a gifted Boston player
named Joe Wilson who didn't make it to Holy Cross that year. With his
bruising physique and incredible speed, Wilson had the makings of a
future star, but he lacked the academic standing to gain admission to
Holy Cross. Brooks had encouraged Wilson to spend a year at a nearby
Catholic school, Assumption Prep, to bolster his academic foundation
so that he could make an easier transition to Holy Cross the following
year. The new dean argued to his colleagues that what Wilson really
lacked was not intellectual ability but a setting in which people encouraged him to study. The young man had been so good at football, Brooks
suspected, that he had simply let his schoolwork slide. The coaches
clearly wanted Wilson, but Brooks cared about more than recruiting the
best players. The last thing he wanted was for a black student to make
such a risky, high-profile move, only to flunk out of Holy Cross.

Those first summer practices were more brutal than anything Jenkins
had experienced in high school. He thought the coach was crazy for
making them run so many laps in the heat, but he stayed quiet about it:
He wasn't going to let anyone hear him complain about being worked
too hard. Secretly he couldn't wait until classes started, when there
would be some relief from days devoted to football.

Meals, at least, were something to look forward to. For many of the
students, whatever their background, the quality of food at Holy Cross
was a pleasant surprise. Kimball Dining Hall had a reputation for serving up some of the best college meals in the Northeast. The menu regularly featured such items as swordfish, fresh salads, and freshly baked
rolls. The desserts were all homemade. And the building itself was physically impressive, with long mahogany tables, high ceilings, and large
windows. Instead of lining up at a buffet, the men would be served their
meals family-style by student waiters. To Jenkins it felt more like a res-

taurant than a college cafeteria. And he discovered that the football team had special privileges. Not only did the players get their own table in the dining hall, but they were regularly treated to luxuries like steak that were rarely available to other students. Someone somewhere must have decided that they needed the extra protein, he assumed, but it felt more like a badge of honor than a necessary part of training.

One evening after practice, Jenkins struck up a conversation with a black student waiter. Clarence Thomas had also arrived early on campus, as part of a work-study program, earning $1.10 an hour as a waiter. Brooks had helped to set up the job, remembering his own days as a dishwasher at Kimball, earning 33 cents a meal. Thomas didn't like the job, less because of the hard work than the mild indignity of serving other students, but he'd certainly experienced worse. When Jenkins introduced himself, Thomas seemed surprised and pleased to see another black student. He admired athletes and considered himself to be an accomplished one. He and Jenkins immediately hit it off, trading jokes as he worked. Thomas came across to Jenkins as jovial and good-natured, not short on opinions but easily moved to a booming laugh.

The two of them began to hang out together on a small hill near the dining hall, drinking cheap wine and talking about their routes to Holy Cross. Jenkins quickly learned of Thomas's anger about the racism and hypocrisy of the Catholic Church, and found it odd that someone so disillusioned with the Church should have picked a Catholic college. But the anger didn't seem to overwhelm the sophomore, or overshadow the benefits of being at Holy Cross. Jenkins suspected that Thomas, like him, had found it impossible to turn down the offer of a free education. And there were other things to talk about, from black activists to their shared love of sports. Growing up in Savannah, Thomas's basketball skills had earned him the nickname "Cousy," after Bob Cousy, a famed Boston Celtics star and Holy Cross graduate. But he thought his talents on the football field were pretty good, too, having played on his high school team. When Thomas jokingly boasted that he could probably run circles around the football team, Jenkins challenged him to prove it and the sophomore immediately agreed.

When the two of them met on the field for a casual scrimmage, Jenkins was immediately struck by how different Thomas looked out of his waiter uniform. His hair was uncombed. He wore combat boots and army fatigues. Thomas also proved to be quite talented at football. He could throw a ball at least sixty-five yards and run fast. Jenkins just wasn't so sure the man could take a hit, mentally or physically. You needed a certain kind of stamina to keep going when you got hurt. After a vigorous back-and-forth, Jenkins walked away feeling that Thomas was more like the guys he'd played with in his old neighborhood than someone he'd encounter on the Holy Cross team. Looking back, Thomas laughs and agrees with Jenkins's assessment, saying, "I could probably do everything but take a hit." At the time, though, Jenkins recalls the sophomore looking slightly miffed.

Still, having heard about Thomas's ability, Tom Boisture invited the sophomore to try out for the team as a walk-on. While Thomas says he declined, Boisture recalled the young man coming out for a practice. The first thing Boisture noticed when Thomas walked onto the field was that the sophomore had likely borrowed someone's shoes, since they seemed much too big for his feet. And while Thomas may have acted boisterous around fellow students like Jenkins, he showed a different side of himself to the head football coach. Thomas was more introverted than Boisture had expected, and he looked a little sad. He clearly had physical talent and the kind of drive Boisture often worked years to nurture in his players. Whether Thomas saw his one outing as a tryout or simply a scrimmage, he didn't make the team. When Boisture looked around to talk to him, the young athlete was gone. Like Jenkins, Boisture suspected that Thomas wasn't one to take failure easily.

The rest of the students began to arrive on Labor Day weekend. Jenkins was chatting with a student at his Beaven Hall residence when another family pushed open the door onto his floor. The doors were among the first things Jenkins had liked about the dorm. They swung like the ones in an Old West saloon, letting everyone make a grand entrance. A tall, lanky white student with a mustache and tousled hair came through, followed by his parents. When they entered Jenkins's room, he strained to hear their conversation: "Hmm. That's interesting. Who's that?" Jenkins realized they were talking about the Nancy Wilson album covers on his side of the room. Maybe they hadn't heard of Wilson? Then he realized that the parents weren't really interested in his favorite singer: They were just figuring out that their son was sharing his room with a black man.

When Jenkins walked into the room, his roommate introduced himself as Tom Anderson. Although Anderson was about the same height as Jenkins, he looked to be at least thirty pounds lighter. He was enrolled as a pre-med student but harbored a secret love of writing. Anderson, it turned out, had been asked about rooming with a black student. He simply hadn't bothered to tell his parents.

Holy Cross had called up white students and, in some cases, mailed out letters over the summer to ask if they would mind rooming with a black man. Nobody was quite sure who had suggested the strategy, and the approach was poorly executed; some of the students who ended up with black roommates hadn't been asked in advance. None of the black students were asked about their preferences. To Father Brooks, who learned of it after the fact, the move seemed ham-handed at best. While he didn't want any black student in a dorm situation where he'd feel unwelcome, Brooks didn't like the idea of anyone at Holy Cross offering white freshmen a chance to reject someone based on his skin color. It undermined the college's values to even ask the question, as if discomfort were valid grounds for discrimination, and not asking black students the same question was proof that their discomfort didn't matter.

For all his anger over racism, Thomas, for one, didn't mind rooming with a white man. He had been assigned to live in a residence called Hanselman, and his roommate was John Siraco, who had transferred from Northwestern University. Siraco was a dogged worker, which suited Thomas just fine. Thomas wasn't interested in socializing with his roommate or hanging out with him to listen to music. He mainly wanted to put his head down and work. He was studying English, which had never been his strongest subject, but he thought he might one day become a journalist. More important, perhaps, he wanted to shed the vestiges of the Gullah dialect he had spoken as a child in coastal Georgia, so he could seamlessly blend—at least vocally—with his college peers.

Like Thomas, Ed Jones came to campus alone, having made his way up from Washington, D.C., on the bus. The idea that his mother might have accompanied him to Worcester was so ridiculous that it had never occurred to him to ask her. The only time Jones had really been in a school residence was as a child, when he and his sister were briefly sent to live in a Maryland children's center, along with their disabled brother. His mother had been admitted to the hospital, although he was never quite sure why. The complex seemed to house everyone from mentally handicapped kids and orphans to juvenile delinquents, many of whom were black. Jones vividly recalled some young caregivers there who had presented him with a pile of used shoes to pick through, but he couldn't find his size. Now he was walking into a residence as a college student, wearing a perfectly sized pair of shoes on his feet, the ones he had picked up during the riot that followed King's death.

Jones felt people staring at him as he headed to his dorm room. He knew that his clothes didn't look out of place; the days of wearing ties and jackets were rapidly giving way to denim and tie-dyed shirts. He was dressed just like everyone else. The only remarkable thing about him, he figured, was the color of his skin.

Jones's roommate was a white math major from Fall River, Massachusetts. Jones assumed they were rooming together because his roommate was also planning to major in math—he couldn't see what else would have brought them together. Jones tried to get used to the feel of his new home. The bed had crisp cotton sheets, the pale blank walls looked freshly painted, and the corridors were filled with laughter as his roommate dashed in and out of the room. Students from the same prep schools had been placed together, and everyone seemed to know one another. Along with the wait service in the dining halls, there was maid service in the residences, which made Jones think about his mother. She could have worked in a place like this, tidying up after rowdy boys who were drunk with their first taste of freedom. She might even have enjoyed it. The thought of that made him smile.

Despite the looks that Jones had gotten on his way up to his room, nobody seemed curious to know much about him. He wondered if maybe they sensed that he was a poor student on a scholarship. It was hard to know for certain, of course, and, anyway, Jones wasn't much interested in reaching out to the other students. His hallmates struck him as ambitious up-and-comers, future lawyers and doctors and businessmen who knew exactly why they'd come to Holy Cross. Jones, who had no clear idea what his future might look like, realized how isolated he was going to be, but he also wondered if maybe he preferred it that way. In some ways he liked to be left alone. After so many moves in his childhood, he had largely stopped making the effort to meet people he didn't know. Nevertheless, he felt it would have been nice if someone had reached out to him. No one did. It was more than a week before he discovered that another black man lived at the end of the corridor.

Jones wasn't sure how long he would last at Holy Cross. Sitting alone in his dorm room, he thought about the anticipation he had felt months earlier on the car trip with Father Brooks. There had been camaraderie, a clear sense from the jokes and the banter that they were welcome. That feeling was missing now. He carefully unpacked the books he had brought, and the clothes that his mother had washed and folded before he left. He preferred reading to conversation; listening to talking. But it gnawed at him that he was so clearly being left out. And it was also clear to him that some questioned his right to be there. It wasn't long before one of the white students asked the question Jones assumed was on everybody else's mind: "Is it easy to get in here if you're colored?" He felt so diminished and ridiculed by the question that he had no response, but he later wrote about his anger in an article in *The Crusader*. Maybe, because of Brooks, it had arguably become easy for some of them to get in because of their skin color. But the question itself showed why it wouldn't be easy to stay.

One person Jones felt a connection with was Gil Hardy. The two of them met once classes started. Like Jones, Hardy was serious and he was a big reader. Jones hoped that the two of them might become good friends. Clarence Thomas also found himself drawn to Hardy. Thomas liked the Philadelphia native's drive and obvious intelligence. Hardy had studied Greek, Latin, and French in high school and decided to take some second-year courses from the start at Holy Cross. He seemed less concerned about maintaining high grades than keeping himself challenged, and he would often come back from class eager to share some piece of knowledge or discussion he'd had with a professor. If Hardy felt any particular disadvantages in being black, he rarely talked about them. He certainly didn't seem to let it shape his ambitions. Thomas envied Hardy's optimism and his warmth toward everyone. He was the kind of man everyone would want for a friend.

It was tougher for Thomas to bond with many of the other black students at first, in part because there were so few opportunities to formally interact. They were in different classes during the day and went home to different residences at night. While other black students might nod when they passed him on campus—in recognition or sympathy, he couldn't be sure—nobody had the time for long conversations between classes. Thomas liked Jenkins, having connected with the smooth-talking football player over the summer, but their interactions were often superficial. From where Thomas sat, Jenkins wasn't a man who seemed to take life all that seriously, and he seemed used to being the center of attention. Jenkins certainly hadn't grown up with an exhausted mother who couldn't cope and had left her son to be raised in a harsh, demanding household where love came in the form of discipline and idleness was a sin. And Thomas's childhood hadn't been filled with block parties and baseball games, a warm, gregarious mother, and a father who never let his own struggles interfere with his bonds to his children. Jenkins might not be able to match Thomas's academic performance, but he didn't seem to hold that as an ambition. Thomas found himself envying the easy laugh and gregarious style of the freshman athlete. Even so, Thomas didn't find it hard to make friends in his classes. Whatever turmoil Thomas may have battled because of his skin color, he didn't harbor any grudges against the white students. He liked them and quickly made several good friends.

Ted Wells was an enigma. Like Jenkins, he had the confidence of a man who was comfortable with where he was from. But Wells also had an obvious ambition and desire to be respected for his intelligence, a trait that Thomas shared. Where they differed, perhaps, was in approach: While Wells seemed to enjoy the intellectual challenge of his classes, Thomas was more methodical in doing what needed to be done. More important, perhaps, each man had very different reactions to the racial inequality around them. Wells, having grown up in a city that had become a mecca and marching ground for black pride, was looking for ways to re-create that sense of brotherhood at Holy Cross. Thomas had spent much of his life digesting racism on his own. He had learned to move easily in the white community, even if he never felt a part of it, and he didn't have much interest in making skin color the prime factor in determining his social circle. Thomas wanted to be seen as someone who could fit in and get along with anybody. Let Wells revel in the black identity and push for civil rights. What bothered Thomas wasn't being black; it was being noticed for being black.

Thomas resigned himself to focusing primarily on his classes and his job in Kimball Dining Hall. He knew he could handle the academic load after the grind of seminary life. What he didn't know was where he'd feel happy. There were now a handful of black kids in his second-year class of 550 students. He liked having white and black friends, and he made a deliberate effort to get along with everyone. He had hoped that Holy Cross would be a fresh start, a place where he could just be himself. But after a few weeks he began to suspect that it would be a place to be endured, not enjoyed. He didn't feel the warm embrace of belonging, and his disappointment compounded his anger. At times, though, he found himself forgetting about the issues in his life. When swept up in a conversation or sharing a joke, he showed an enthusiasm that stuck with many of his classmates. Thomas's laugh soon became famous as perhaps the loudest one on campus.

Others had made an easier adjustment. Despite a fierce case of allergies—the worst he had ever experienced—Grayson was enjoying the kind of welcome afforded to new athletes. He began to meet the various members of the basketball team, including a white freshman on scholarship named Buddy Venne, an impressive shooter and all-state player who would become one of Grayson's closest friends. Grayson was aware that he drew stares on campus, but it didn't bother him much. His height and skin color had made him stand out in his white high school, too, and it hadn't stopped him from being one of the most popular students there. It was certainly a new experience to be living with a white roommate, Thomas A. Fulham, Jr., who smoked cigars and played the Mamas & the Papas every night in their room. His own tastes ran more to Motown. But he'd cope. Grayson hadn't come this far by raising a stink every time he felt a twinge of discomfort. If there were going to be complaints about how poorly Holy Cross integrated its black students into campus life, they weren't going to come from Grayson. He had learned to just get along.

As they approached the fall of 1968, Father Brooks made a point of telling many of his colleagues how lucky the college was to have wooed such high achievers. But he could sense that the transition was going to be tougher for the black students than he'd imagined. It wasn't just the threat of racism that worried him, since most of the black men had had ample experience in dealing with that in their hometowns. What worried him were the academic demands. He had found Holy Cross challenging himself, despite the rigorous high school education he had received at Boston Latin School. The Jesuits prided themselves on making life tougher, not easier, for the young men under their charge. While many freshmen found the adjustment jolting, Brooks suspected it might be tougher for those who came in under greater scrutiny and pressure than many of their peers.

He quietly checked in with some of the professors to see if any of the black students seemed to be having particular difficulty in adjusting. He'd often stop to chat with those students he'd met and recruited the previous spring, and ask them about their workload, their living situation, and their extracurriculars. His goal was less to be their friend than to help remind them of what it would take to succeed. Even the brightest of the recruits would face extra hurdles, he believed, from the affront of low expectations from professors to the chill of being made to feel they didn't belong.

But Brooks was certain that they would make it. He had met most of them and had seen the ambition in their eyes. He had seen in them the quickness and depth that he looked for in every student coming to Holy Cross. These men weren't going to crumble under social pressure; most of them had likely been dealing with it for most of their lives. It was sweat and nerves that had helped Brooks get through the long months of running a repeater station in rural France during the war to help keep communications flowing for General Patton's army, and his faith that had helped him endure frigid cold during the Battle of the Bulge. Intelligence was the easy part. They all had that. The measure of a man was how hard he was willing to work for what he wanted, and he could see that these young men were hungry.

Still, Brooks knew he had to make an extra effort to help them succeed. Nothing heroic; he just wanted to let them know that he was there to listen, even if they weren't interested in talking. He wanted to keep them on track, the way he did for every student he talked to. For all their bravado and pride and accomplishments, the students entering their first year were just kids. And they were arriving just as many of the old norms of how to behave were falling away. The college was starting to bend on its traditional rules about drinking and having female visitors in the dorms. Expectations about how to dress were changing. The concept of having a mandatory core curriculum was under debate. The Jesuits no longer even forced students to attend church. Whether the students would find the newly relaxed rules liberating remained to be seen, but it certainly made for a less stable environment.

It was a different world from when Brooks had enrolled in the fall of 1942 at the age of nineteen. Back then, Holy Cross had felt almost like a cocoon, with its stringent rules and clear-cut road map to success. But within months of his arrival, Brooks had been shipped off to war. By the time he made it back to Holy Cross four years later, the climate had changed. With a flood of veterans streaming back onto campus, the students weren't boys anymore; they had come back with life experiences that would forever shape them. The focus was now on moving forward. America had won the war, and the country was flush with optimism.

Two decades later such optimism seemed to be in short supply. Brooks could see that many students had grown distrustful of people like him in the administration, wary of any sign of condescension. Brooks knew himself well enough to realize that his blunt manner could intimidate even his colleagues. He wasn't one to ask questions and nurture egos. His own sisters liked to joke about how strong-willed he was, how even they didn't want to get on his bad side. He knew that most freshmen would have neither the courage nor the inclination to approach a middle-aged college administrator. So he would have to go to them.

FIVE

Winds of Change

The black students had come to Holy Cross with an acute awareness of three basic facts about the school: It was white, Catholic, and all male. But the college also had a rich history when it came to both race and social justice. From the start, Holy Cross had set itself apart from the city of Worcester, occupying a commanding hilltop position. When the school's founder, Benedict J. Fenwick, had come upon the Pakachoag tribe's "Hill of Pleasant Springs," he was thrilled with the location, declaring in 1843 that "there is not one [location] to surpass it in the United States." However, the school's geography merely reinforced what the town's working-class residents perceived as smugness. They weren't entirely wrong. Fenwick, a portly, Maryland-born Jesuit who was bishop of Boston, had been looking to establish a Jesuit college in New England that would cater exclusively to Catholic students. It was an odd mission for a man educated at Georgetown University, which was open to all faiths, but Fenwick wanted to create a school that would produce future priests, and a place where students could be free from the rising chorus of anti-Catholic sentiment, which was particularly pronounced around the Boston area. A massive influx of Irish Roman Catholic immigrants in the early nineteenth century had changed the makeup of the city, and the immigrants were blamed for bringing wages down and taxes up, as well as for being violent and spreading diseases like tuberculosis and cholera. There were dozens of popular anti-Catholic publications, which ran lurid tales of convent life that featured allegations of slaughtered babies and promiscuous priests (a hoax perpetrated most famously by a Montreal prostitute-turned-author named Maria Monk) and articles about the Vatican's alleged conspiracy to "take over the world." In 1834 a mob burned an Ursuline convent and school just outside Boston. Three years later, a run-in between British firefighters and the members of an Irish funeral procession sparked a massive riot.

Because of the anti-Catholic sentiment plaguing Boston, Fenwick had good reason to look outside the city in his search for land. As a thriving industrial city with easy access to Boston, New York, and Providence, Worcester fit the bill. He chose a charismatic, controversial, big-bellied Jesuit named Thomas F. Mulledy as the college's first president. Prior to his arrival at the College of the Holy Cross in 1843, Mulledy was best known for his scandal-plagued tenure as a leader of the Church's Maryland "province," where he had been in charge of selling off the Jesuit order's slaves, on the condition that he found new owners who would agree to respect their "religious needs" and family bonds. The Jesuits had deemed slavery to be divinely ordained, a practice that enabled the Church to claim to protect poor black families by placing slaves in the hands of a benevolent owner. Emancipation was seen as tantamount to abandoning people who couldn't care for themselves. But the financial cost of maintaining slave families, if not the moral one, began to weigh on the Jesuit community. When Mulledy allowed many of the slave families to be split apart and resold to Protestant orders, several of his colleagues were openly outraged.

Among the first students to enroll at Holy Cross were four sons of Michael Morris Healy, an Irish-born planter in Georgia, and Eliza Clark, a mixed-race slave whom Healy owned and had fallen in love with. Their children were considered slaves, making them ineligible to attend school in the South. Instead James, Patrick, Hugh, and Sherwood Healy came to Holy Cross in 1844. The Healy boys did well—Patrick went on to become president of Georgetown University in 1874, James was valedictorian of the first graduating class in 1849 and later became the country's first African American Catholic bishop, Michael became a celebrated sea captain, and Sherwood became a priest and rector of Boston's Cathedral of the Holy Cross.

John Brooks believed that the college's history demonstrated the power that a Holy Cross education could have. The Healy brothers had thrived against daunting odds and had gone on to achieve great things. Brooks looked to the legacy of the Healy brothers when he thought of Holy Cross's role in educating black men; he believed, in fact, that all colleges had an obligation to reach out to black students, though they were largely failing on that front. In the fall of 1968, *Newsweek* estimated that 275,000 black undergraduates were enrolled in U.S. campuses out of a total population of 6.5 million undergrads, and more than half of those students were enrolled at one of the 111 predominantly "Negro colleges" concentrated in the South. Most of the remaining students were enrolled at large state schools. Black students were still an anomaly at small liberal arts colleges.

During Art Martin's two years at Holy Cross, he had been treated as the invisible man. The other students were friendly, but it was a polite form of civility. Few of his fellow students had ever asked about his background or his beliefs. It was almost as if they were pretending he was one of the guys when everyone knew that he would never really fit in. Now, in his junior year, he was getting a different kind of look as he walked around. It wasn't the occasional what-are-you-doing-here glance of semesters past. With more than two dozen other black students on campus, the fact that he was black suddenly seemed to give him a new identity. Martin had become part of a group. Other students started asking him about black power and Malcolm X. They began to acknowledge, however awkwardly, that he had unique insights to offer.

The sudden presence of other black men was liberating for Martin. He grew an Afro and wore a dashiki. Before, it hadn't even occurred to him to express his tastes and heritage. In previous years he had been focused on just trying to get through each day. Now that there were so many other black students on campus, he felt more comfortable standing out.

Like the rest of the country, Holy Cross had entered a new era. While many of the professors still liked to joke that the faculty was far more liberal than the students, a ripple of revolution was slowly making its way to Worcester. Cutoff jeans, sandals, and shoulder-length hair had become more common sights in the classroom. Peace signs and mind-altering drugs were now a part of campus life, and the aroma of marijuana wafted through the residence halls. The activist group Students for a Democratic Society had set up a vigorous chapter at Holy Cross. Although less inclined toward violence than some other SDS chapters, the Worcester group was vocal in everything from blocking Marine recruitment on campus to demonstrating against the Vietnam War. For young men raised in middle-class homes with Virgin Mary statues in every room, it was a heady change of pace.

The faculty was doing its part to further the burgeoning revolution. The incoming students had been assigned to read Michael Harrington's jolting *The Other America: Poverty in the United States* over the summer. As dean, Brooks thought it would get the students thinking about what was going on across the country. Brooks had particular respect for Harrington, a Holy Cross graduate whose book chronicled how millions of Americans were struggling under an insidious form of modern poverty. Harrington described them as trapped in urban ghettos or long-forgotten rural towns, far from the manicured lawns of suburbia and "populated by the failures, by those driven from the land and bewildered by the city, by old people suddenly confronted with the torments of loneliness and poverty, and by minorities facing a wall of prejudice." Moreover, the poor were surrounded by middle-class brethren who no longer understood that poverty existed, in part because cheap mass-market clothing had enabled people of all income levels to dress alike. In twentieth-century

America, Harrington concluded, the poor had no political voice because they had no presence.

Harrington's argument resonated with many of the black students, but people like Ted Wells didn't feel as helpless as Harrington suggested. In his world the poor and the disenfranchised were starting to be heard. Wells had certainly felt the influence of black power in Washington and would sometimes sneak off to rallies near the White House. He understood the issues that people were fighting for, and he felt very comfortable giving his own opinions about them. Living in an all-black neighborhood hadn't left Wells feeling marginalized. His teachers were black, his coaches were black, and most of his heroes were black, too. He rarely had to deal with racism because he rarely came into contact with racists. He was acutely aware of the barriers and injustices that black Americans were facing across the country, but when it came to his own life, Wells was used to having a voice.

Holy Cross, however, proved to be a trickier landscape than he'd expected. Suddenly Wells had to navigate a culture in which he was the outsider. If he was going to spend the next four years there, he needed to find a way to thrive. He struck up a friendship with Art Martin, who took on a big brother role, helping many of the black athletes adjust to life on campus. The two had met through Jenkins and Dickerson, both of whom had met Martin the previous winter when he had shown them around the cold, muddy campus. Wells liked Martin's energy and his conviction that the group of black men should make their presence felt on campus. Wells was deeply interested in the intense debate over achieving racial equality that was raging on every campus. He wasn't sure yet if he supported working within the system, as King had advocated, or adopting the more militant and separatist stance that leaders such as Stokely Carmichael urged. Wells had also bonded with Jenkins and Dickerson at football practice, and had gotten to know Grayson through the athletics department, but the black students' interactions were sporadic and didn't fully compensate for the loneliness of adjusting to a strange environment. Something had to change.

Art Martin, energized by his new sense of identity, started talking to Bob DeShay and Wells about the idea of forming a black student union. Martin had been craving some sort of community for years, and now that there were more than a handful of black students, he saw his opportunity to create one. Although he had been student council president at his largely white all-boys high school in New Jersey, he had never considered seeking a formal leadership role at Holy Cross. But now there was a chance to finally have an impact on a college that had been largely immune to the calls for black power spreading across the country, to raise consciousness about the kinds of injustices that had spurred riots in his hometown of Newark the year before. DeShay, whose sympathies lay with groups like SDS, liked the idea of shaking up the old guard in Worcester. Similar unions were coming together at colleges across the country; Holy Cross needed one of its own.

When Martin mentioned the idea to Brooks, the dean was supportive. A formal union would likely need funding and the support of a faculty adviser, and he wasn't sure what the mission of the group might be. Still, Brooks wanted the college to support any initiative that might make the black students feel more at ease and empowered.

Wells, for one, felt excited by the prospect of a formal black student union. Although he had kept up a brave face and confident demeanor since coming to Holy Cross, the sudden sense of isolation had been hard to take. He was eager to bring the black students together, both to hang out and to present a united front to the administration on a range of issues. The fact that he had arrived at the college just a few weeks earlier didn't matter. He had taken on leadership roles in the past, and it felt natural to do so again. Besides, the freshman class alone had more than tripled the size of the school's black population. He knew a BSU wouldn't have even been possible the year before.

In early October they met in a room at the Hogan Campus Center. One or two of the older black students had chosen not to come, citing conflicts, though Art Martin suspected they didn't want to associate themselves with any black cause. The goal was to form a group that could formally raise issues with Father Brooks, from white bias in the curriculum to the absence of any black faculty at the school. Martin took the lead and started writing out by hand a constitution and bylaws for the new Black Student Union. When Thomas mentioned that he had a typewriter, they quickly decided that he would type up the founding document. The list of demands being debated was long: black faculty, courses in black history and literature, black-themed events, representation, a budget, transportation to extend their social lives beyond the white campus, and, of course, many more black students. The men were divided over how much the group should demand and how confrontational they should be. Most of them were, after all, getting a free education from the college they were now complaining about. But that fact didn't really have much impact on the motivations of young men who had been watching civil rights battles play out on their TV screens and in their communities. They weren't about to celebrate what the college had done right at a time when so much in the world was wrong.

If some in the administration had expected the black students to feel nothing but gratitude for their scholarships, they were mistaken. Within weeks of arriving at Holy Cross, a number of the recruits were feeling frustrated about everything from the workload to the atmosphere in their dorms. Some had shared their complaints already with Brooks; many had not. Without proof that other students were facing similar difficulties, they didn't want to look like the only ones who weren't able to cope. For Thomas there was another dimension to the angst. On the Sunday of his second week on campus, he decided to go to Mass. Having gone to church regularly for most of his life, it felt like second nature. But something had snapped since he had left the seminary. Soon after the priest got up to expand on the readings during the homily, Thomas got up and walked out. During the rest of his time at Holy Cross, Thomas never went to Mass again. The faith that had been so much a part of his life for so long was gone, or at least pushed back to a place where he wouldn't acknowledge it.

At that first BSU meeting, Jones watched as Thomas and several others jostled for attention. While their fledgling membership would barely fill two lunch tables, he could see cliques already beginning to form. The only thing all of the members knew they had in common was their skin color. The Philadelphia contingent stuck together; the athletes were already tight-knit and prone to joking around; the Savannah boys, especially Thomas, struck Jones as bellicose and argumentative. Everyone seemed passionate about their agenda, yet Ed Jones wasn't convinced that any of their ideas would be put into action. Why would anyone listen seriously to their demands? "Below our blackness," Jones would write a year later in *The Crusader,* "was our natural handicap of being human beings with various viewpoints and we had bitter arguments with excruciating results from the very beginning."

Still, the BSU's common desire to drive radical change at Holy Cross—a school that had already left many of them feeling intimidated and small—brought them together. They felt part of something bigger, part of a movement that was inspiring students to demonstrate not just at Holy Cross and other American campuses but in practically every part of the world. The Northern Irish resistance to British rule and anti-Soviet protests in Poland and Czechoslovakia showed that disenfranchised people were embracing their rights. Feminism, socialism, and black oppression had become part of everyday conversation. The young felt increasingly powerful, convinced that the world was on the cusp of change. In that environment, even two dozen black men attending a conservative white college could see the power they might wield if they came together.

Grayson found the early BSU meetings immensely enjoyable. It was like watching theater. There was an immediate friction, sometimes good-natured, sometimes not, between Thomas and Wells. If one said yes, the other almost automatically said no. While Thomas was initially reticent at meetings, he soon started to spar with Wells over various ideas. Rarely did Thomas himself ever suggest an idea; he merely liked to shoot them down. Grayson sensed that Wells was speaking from his heart, but he often wondered if Thomas was being contrarian just to keep things lively. One minute Thomas preached solidarity and brotherhood; the next he would launch a blistering attack against other students for assuming that all black students had to think alike. But Thomas also pointed to a very real problem: As the roomful of mostly teenagers began to articulate what they needed to make the school livable, the list kept getting longer.

Thomas argued that the group had to focus on what they needed instead of what they wanted. They decided that they needed a vehicle so that they could go off campus to meet black women. They needed an office, money, black professors, and black authors in the curriculum, not to mention more black students. Grayson wanted to remove the reference to "Old Black Joe" from the school's beloved rallying song, "Mamie Reilly. " They wanted Holy Cross to take a stronger stance against the Vietnam War, which was putting too many brothers into body bags; many of the men feared they might be called to fight.

That first meeting, though hardly decisive, set the structure of the BSU. Thomas agreed to become the correspondence secretary. Martin would be the president and Wells would be second in charge. There wasn't much competition for the leadership roles. Though many of the freshmen had met and liked Brooks, they didn't particularly want to be spending time with people in the administration, and the older students were too focused on keeping up their grades to take on heavy responsibilities. Everyone decided that Martin and Wells would represent the group together since Wells was so persuasive and Martin was a junior who already had a relationship with the dean.

When Martin told Brooks about the outcome of the first meeting, the priest immediately suggested a dinner meeting with the president. He wanted Father Swords to hear about the black students' experience and have a chance to share his own views with Wells and Martin. Brooks knew that the group had strength in its unity, but he also knew that they would need a direct line to the administration or else their requests would likely fall on deaf ears. With demonstrations against the war and calls for change coming from other groups on campus, the BSU could easily become part of the cacophony. Brooks felt the college had a special responsibility to the black students. It may have taken a risk in bringing some of them in, but the students had also taken a risk in agreeing to come. Issues like Vietnam and poverty were important but largely beyond his control; the steps that Holy Cross could take to promote civil rights and the success of its black students on campus were not.

Brooks immediately warmed to Wells when Martin introduced him at their dinner that fall. Behind the young man's composure, Brooks sensed a quick and curious mind. He asked Wells what he was planning to do when he finished school, and how he was doing so far in his classes. Brooks started most conversations with students that way: a mild grilling on academics, followed by questions about their ambitions. He never wanted them to forget why they were enrolled. Wells didn't have a concrete answer. Law school was an option, but he was also interested in business school or perhaps in pursuing a Ph.D. All he knew at that point was that his academic ambitions extended beyond getting an undergraduate degree at Holy Cross.

The conversation was a bit stilted at the start. Swords had indicated before the meeting that he was willing to listen to what the students wanted, but Brooks could see that the president wasn't terribly happy with the concept of a black student union. The name immediately evoked images of black power and angry rhetoric, not to mention the demonstrations that had been disrupting campuses across the Northeast. Holy Cross was already dealing with its own chapter of Students for a Democratic Society. The last thing the president wanted was another angry student group that might issue demands and stir up trouble.

It didn't help, then, that Martin and Wells began the dinner by asking for an office and a budget, a modest one to start. Brooks was impressed by their negotiating skills: The two had already established an informal good cop/bad cop dynamic between them. Wells would go for what Martin saw as the outlandish proposal—the big money, the audacious position—and Martin would be the one to suggest a compromise that reflected what they actually expected to get.

Brooks enjoyed a good debate, and he wanted to delve into the various points to explain what the school could and couldn't do, but Swords didn't like the idea of negotiating with students over perks. Brooks couldn't blame him. He would never have dared to ask for special privileges from a college president when he was a student. A year or two earlier, it would have been unusual to see that kind of behavior in the student body. But much had changed in the past year, and the black students weren't the only ones with demands and requests. Swords's answer to Wells and Martin was the same as the one he gave to any other student organization: He would do his best to accommodate their needs. The reality was that Holy Cross didn't have a lot of extra cash, with an operating budget that barely covered costs and an endowment that was hovering below $6 million.

Swords made it clear that he preferred Brooks to handle the demands of the BSU. The president largely deferred to his colleague on matters relating to student life, and it was Brooks who had insisted the college aggressively recruit black students. It was Brooks who had skirted the rules to get some of them in. He would have to be the one to acclimatize his recruits to the school's harsh realities. Swords also knew it was a role that Brooks was going to take on, whether he was asked to do it or not.

Wells and Martin both believed that having Brooks as their main contact would work to the BSU's advantage, and they were right. Although Brooks was acutely aware of the budget constraints, he tried to fulfill as many of the BSU's requests as possible. He wasn't motivated only by a desire to make the men feel more at ease, though that certainly played a role because a lot of his peers were looking at the black students as some sort of test case for Holy Cross. If the young men failed, it would fuel the argument that they should never have been invited. Brooks also believed that much of what the students wanted was reasonable. He, too, wanted the faculty and curriculum to reflect the experiences of the broader population. And he needed the experience to succeed. He had already started an ambitious recruitment drive across the Northeast in the hope of at least doubling the number of black freshmen in the fall of 1969.

Brooks thoroughly enjoyed the dinner with Wells and Martin, and they agreed to make it a monthly meeting. As the two students talked about their experiences on and off campus, Brooks became aware of issues he hadn't anticipated. The men were desperate to get off campus on weekends, both to meet black women at other colleges and to find other social outlets. Holy Cross's movie nights and residence parties seemed to revolve around beer—a distinct second, in the minds of several black students, to wine—and music the black students didn't like. Some of the men had taken to borrowing a car from one accommodating Jesuit professor until Jenkins drove a group to Boston one night and didn't return the car until early the next morning. After that the priest suggested they get their own vehicle. Within weeks of their first dinner, Brooks authorized the purchase of a used burgundy Ford Fairlane station wagon.

Wells and Martin also brought forward the BSU's complaint about the racist lyrics in the school song. Brooks found that harder to address: Holy Cross students had been belting out "Mamie Reilly" for generations. He himself had been singing the song for years without much thought. The lyrics were self-consciously silly, the kind that appealed to mildly drunk sports fans and nostalgic alumni. But the BSU thought the

Art Martin and Ted Wells at a BSU meeting

reference to "Old Black Joe" sounded like a throwback to the days of slavery and Jim Crow. Grayson, in particular, winced every time he heard the lyrics: "Slide Kelly, Slide / Casey's at the bat / Oh, Mamie Reilly, where'd you get that hat? / Down in Old Kentucky / From Old Black Joe." Brooks insisted that it was a tradition, albeit from a different era; tampering with a beloved song struck him as a rash move, especially given the heightened sensitivities of alumni and faculty. However, he agreed to consider it. Now that the men had pointed out what the lyrics meant to them, he could see why the words were offensive.

Amid the lively give-and-take of those initial discussions, Wells discovered his strengths again. He had just arrived at Holy Cross and already he was having dinner with the president of the college! While that was an ego boost in itself, Wells found himself drawn to Brooks, who was a force of life—vibrant, extroverted, and a straight shooter. The dean could talk passionately about religion, sports, and the latest films coming out of Europe. To Wells he seemed a Renaissance man. And Wells could tell that the dean was truly comfortable with them, whereas the president perhaps wasn't. Meeting Brooks gave Wells a more nuanced view of the administration. Maybe it wasn't so conservative and resistant to change. He looked forward to meeting with Brooks again.

Brooks encouraged his colleagues to meet with the black students as often as possible. It was important to make sure that the BSU felt they were being listened to, and important for the people running the college to understand this group of young men. Several faculty members shared Brooks's view that the college had a stake in the success of the students, but they interacted with the men differently than Brooks. While Brooks shared laughs and easy debates with Wells, other administrators found their interactions with the young man to be more somber.

One administration official wrote a memo to the president after dining alone with Wells in February 1969, noting Wells's complaint that the curriculum wasn't relevant to black students. The administration official also noted that the young man was finding the social climate to be miserable, and went on to speculate that Wells was likely not alone in his sense of isolation. The administrator suggested to Swords that they keep their doors open to the black students and admit their ignorance when it came to understanding the black experience.

Wells was certainly finding the transition to Holy Cross tougher than he had imagined it would be. Academically he was struggling for the first time in his life. Football was distracting him from his schoolwork. He had almost flunked his first round of tests, and he was scared. High school felt so easy in retrospect. Realizing he'd have to put in more effort than he ever had before, Wells began to work late into the night, still rising early each day for classes and practice. He ended the semester with a 3.0 grade point average—a solid showing for a freshman but terrifying to the former honors student. He was working around the clock, and he wasn't sure he could keep the juggling act going for long.

Even so, Wells's biggest challenge was cultural. He had been a popular football player in an all-black school; at Holy Cross he felt noticed but largely ignored. He didn't have the same number of easy friendships he'd had in Washington. The way of talking at Holy Cross was different, the jokes were different, even the style was different—a little less flashy and more button-down for the typical student. While Wells had nothing against the white students, he found himself more drawn to the brothers. Many of the blacks had come from cities, like him, while the whites had grown up in suburbs. There was some intersection of taste with musicians such as Jimi Hendrix and Smokey Robinson, but for the most part the black and the white students seemed poles apart. For the first time in his life, Wells was feeling lonely.

Many of the other black students were struggling, too. For some of them it was no worse than what the average white freshman was experiencing. Even Gil Hardy, who finished the first semester with a stellar grade point average of 3.9, appeared a little shell-shocked by the course load. In addition to having to get used to a rigorous academic schedule, several of the black students also complained to Brooks that they were under extra scrutiny, as if people were waiting to see them fail. Brooks didn't try to convince them otherwise, in part because he suspected they were right. Even Hardy found he had to deal with students who openly assumed he'd gotten into Holy Cross because he was black. As unfair as that felt, the reality was that some of the recruits were unprepared and underperforming, academically, socially, or both. One recruit from Philadelphia was, as the dean jotted in a note to Swords, "running scared." The teen appeared to be diligent but was clearly not effective, staying up late and sleeping in. He had complained of getting "crank calls" from other students and feeling isolated. He seemed to be feeling pressure on all fronts. Even the other black students were getting to him at times, with their ribbing and intensity, and he wasn't eating as often at "the black table" in Kimball Hall. Brooks thought the Philadelphia native was a mess, though the dean made a point to write that he "still smiles—is buoyant— he will come back!!" Brooks noted that the young man had faced personal challenges at home, which the two of them talked about often. He vowed to help him get on a more disciplined schedule and to see him more often. He also suggested that Swords invite the freshman to dinner, which the president did.

The black students may not have been fully prepared for Holy Cross but it was becoming increasingly clear that Holy Cross was woefully unprepared for them. Despite the supportive rhetoric he'd received and the president's clear backing, Brooks felt he had to keep justifying his decision to recruit black students. No effort to help the students, no poor grade, seemed to escape notice. Some colleagues were quick to condemn anything that smacked of special treatment. One science professor responded in outright anger after listening to Brooks talk at one faculty meeting about the black students' situation. In a note to Brooks, he pointed out that blacks were not the only minority groups in the country that were worthy of special consideration; there were numerous others that were every bit as badly off as the Negroes. Moreover, he added,

Brooks was doing nothing to help what he described as the extremely poor pure-blood white Americans. In short, he argued, Brooks's behavior was simply racism in another form.

Brooks became used to dealing with that kind of hostility. He was willing to try to change the views that some colleagues had of black men, but only to a point. He didn't care if they were wrong, and they were wrong, in his view: narrow-minded, superficial, just plain wrong. Black families in America weren't just another minority group like people from Ireland or Indonesia, he argued at one faculty meeting. They had been systematically discriminated against and marginalized for the entire history of the country; they had been bought and sold as property, and the discrimination was continuing. Making sure black students had the same access to educational opportunities as everyone else wasn't a plan that would solve every injustice, but Brooks argued it was the role Holy Cross could play.

Brooks sensed that a number of the black students might need someone other than their friends to talk to if they were feeling that the pressure was too much. Some had forged close relationships with one or two professors, but others had not. He asked psychology professor Paul Rosenkrantz to act as a formal adviser to the BSU. Rosenkrantz was the man whose advice Brooks trusted most. He wasn't a typical hire by any measure; he was a former communist, an electrical engineer and merchant seaman who'd proudly spent his youth as an activist. What he may have lacked in terms of a traditional career path, though, he made up for in excellent academic credentials and solid judgment.

Brooks also told Martin and Wells to let the other BSU members know that they could come by and see him anytime. While he was chatty and engaged with the white students on campus, too, he didn't extend an open invitation to most of them. He wanted the black students to know that they were a priority.

One evening in the autumn of 1968, Thomas came knocking on Brooks's door. He had just stopped by to discuss some classes, but Brooks invited him in and the conversation quickly turned from grades and professors to the Catholic Church. Thomas knew that, in addition to his administrative duties, Brooks ran the theology department. But Brooks seemed accessible and open, more curious about Thomas's decision to leave the seminary than sitting in judgment of it. Brooks asked a few questions but mostly he listened as Thomas unburdened himself. Thomas couldn't find refuge in the confessional booth, having resolved never to go back to church, and yet he felt comforted by this priest, who sat nodding as he spoke about the bitterness he was feeling.

The truth was, despite his cheerful manner and loud opinions, Thomas recalls feeling alienated and disheartened as he went through his sophomore year. Some of his classes and assignments, such as translating French texts into English, were more challenging than he had anticipated. He feared that his marks, though solid, might not be high enough to get him into an Ivy League law school. In truth, he was still among the top in his class. Though Brooks nodded in sympathy, he didn't offer the young man any easy solutions. The only way to succeed, both men intuitively understood, was to focus on the work and get it done. For all his sympathy about Thomas's emotional state—and he could see the genuine pain the man was feeling—Brooks wanted to reinforce the idea that Thomas had to be responsible for his own success. Nobody could take the courses for him or master the schoolwork. If Thomas found something too difficult, together they could talk about his other options. But the decisions and the commitment had to come from him. Thomas appreciated Brooks's high standards and the respect that he felt the priest was giving him. He found himself knocking on Brooks's door quite often to talk about coursework, current affairs, and the comings and goings of campus life. In many ways both men were dissatisfied with the status quo. Brooks's office became as close to an oasis as Thomas could hope to find at Holy Cross.

Ed Jones, meanwhile, had issues of his own to work out. Math wasn't turning out to be his calling. He couldn't even recall why he had picked it as a major. He'd never been especially good at it, or interested in it, and he was close to failing.

Because of his shyness, Jones preferred to sit at the back of the classroom, where he couldn't easily read the blackboard. He assumed no one else could see it, either. It wasn't until Thanksgiving, when he, Dickerson, and Wells were driving to Washington, that he became aware of a problem. He was in the front passenger seat, helping navigate. Dickerson drove through a side street in Connecticut and Jones struggled to make out the words on a street sign. A few feet short of the sign, he figured out the letters and yelled for Dickerson to stop. Dickerson slammed on the brakes. "Man, you need glasses!" That Wednesday, Jones went downtown and bought his first pair.

By the end of the first semester, Jones had a 2.3 grade point average. He began to doubt he would last long enough to earn a degree.

But while Jones may have been discouraged, Brooks continued to believe that the intense, quiet young man from Washington had potential and had been quietly talking to some of his professors. Shortly after Jones's report card arrived, Brooks sent the freshman a note that praised his performance as "good" and encouraged him to keep up the hard work. Jones wondered if Brooks was kidding. He knew that a 2.3 average wouldn't take him very far, and he was certain Brooks was aware of that fact, too. Still, Brooks's note encouraged Jones. One of the most senior administrators at the college had taken the time to look up his report card and write him a letter. The following semester, Jones got a 3.2.

Jones was increasingly drawn to writing. He liked his English professor, a Jesuit named Reverend Healy who wore his cassock to class and often paced around the raised platform where his desk sat. Although Jones rarely talked, he caught the professor's attention. It certainly helped that he wrote all his assignments in longhand, because he didn't own a typewriter, and he would sometimes write up his poetry assignments using different colored ink for each line. He received several A's in the class and liked the fact that his professor cared more about his writing than whether or not he spoke up.

One student who didn't appear all that worried about his grades was Eddie Jenkins, who was neither excelling nor failing, but drifting somewhere in between. He had impressed the other students with his confidence and air of sophistication that seemed to come from growing up in New York City. Jenkins was actually just as nervous as the rest of them, but he had learned to put his mouth to good use; few people were better at bravado than Eddie. Still, Jenkins figured he had plenty of excuses if his grades weren't exactly stellar, as college life was keeping him busy.

Wells had convinced Jenkins to come along with him to join the Air Force ROTC on campus, in part because it got them out of Monday football practice. In addition to earning college credit, Wells reasoned, they would be able to get more studying in because they wouldn't be so exhausted from practice. Moreover, if either of them was drafted to serve in Vietnam, it would be better to go as an officer. In Washington high schools, a year of cadet training was mandatory, which meant that Wells had arrived at Holy Cross knowing how to march and take apart a rifle.

Jenkins didn't care for the spit-and-shine part of the ROTC program, and the routines bored him, but he had great respect for anyone serving in the military, as some of his family had done, and felt proud when he put on the uniform. At Thanksgiving he put it on to hitch a ride home to New York. He knew he looked good—and trustworthy. When he arrived at his home in Queens, his parents were immediately taken aback. Jenkins's older brother was at that point serving in the U.S. Air Force in Vietnam, and here was another boy, home from college in a uniform, like he was acting in a play. His father looked distinctly unimpressed. Feeling ashamed, Jenkins took off the uniform. After the holiday, he returned to Worcester on the bus in civilian clothes.

The ROTC was a controversial institution on campus, in any case, and neither Jenkins nor Wells wanted to think seriously about going to Vietnam. Many of their friends were already off fighting. Within months both men decided to drop out of the ROTC. When they turned in their uniforms and quit, the Air Force major asked why they were leaving the program so soon. They told him that they had decided to leave on principle. They said they didn't support the war.

The officer was clearly not impressed with their explanation. In his memo for the record, he noted that the two cadets were determined to quit the ROTC because the program represented the U.S. military establishment, and therefore represented an agency of the U.S. government that was responsible for the Vietnam conflict. Furthermore, they told him, since this was not a black man's fight and they didn't agree with war, they felt they couldn't belong to any agency of the government that supported it. In short, they were like many of the young men on campus who had decided the ROTC was clearly not for them. Although it bothered him immensely, he felt he had no choice but to let them have their way.

SIX

Love, Liberty, and Learning

Eddie Jenkins, who welcomed weekends as a break from the grind of football and studying, was finding it tough to adjust to the mating rituals at Holy Cross. In particular, it was hard for the freshman to work up much enthusiasm about the "mixer," a weekend event for which busloads of female students from neighboring colleges were brought to campus. Sometimes the mixer was a casual party held on the floor of a residence, but it could also be a formal dance in the Field House. Most of the students on campus seemed to consider the mixers the highlight of campus life. For big draws like Spring Weekend, men would submit photos of their dates to *The Crusader*, which then solicited votes on who was bringing the prettiest girl. Such practices seemed weird and outdated to Jenkins, but what bothered him most was that there were rarely more than a handful of black women on the bus, and hitting on the white girls brought its own set of problems. It wasn't just that some of them apparently failed to find Eddie attractive or seemed nervous about hanging out with a black man. He wanted to meet some sisters and, like some of the other black students, found that there was just too much tension in trying to pick up a white girl. As one student complained at a BSU meeting, the looks from some white classmates implied that the black men were "dirtying up" their women.

The members of the BSU decided they would have to go out and look for women on their own, and Jenkins frequently organized these weekend trips off campus. When the BSU secured its own station wagon, many of the black students often found that when they asked to borrow the "van" that Eddie J. had booked it first. Usually that just meant that they would have to pile in and be prepared to contribute for gas. Most nights, the men would pool coins from their pockets. "That's all you got, man?" someone would yell into the backseat as they pulled into a station. "Come on, dig deep!" Gas station attendants struggled to hold on to the fistfuls of coins that the men would shove at them through the window—often delivered with a smile and the greeting of "Peace, brother!" to dispel the inevitable irritation.

Jenkins discovered that it wasn't hard to find parties at one of the Seven Sisters colleges—Barnard, Bryn Mawr, Mount Holyoke, Radcliffe, Smith, Wellesley, and Vassar. The men also favored Newton College of the Sacred Heart, a Catholic women's school that eventually merged with Boston College in 1974. They found that black women were as eager as they were to socialize, having experienced their own sense of isolation on largely white campuses. They were forming their own black dorms and organizations, too, and were eager to connect with the BSU members at Holy Cross.

Eddie had briefly dated a woman at Anna Maria College named Kathy Ambush but quickly decided that, although she was cute, she was too short for him. They got along so well, though, that he asked her to come along on a trip into Boston with Gil Hardy and Clarence Thomas, hoping to introduce her to "Cous," as many of the men now called Thomas in reference to his childhood nickname. As soon as Jenkins heard the two of them laughing and talking in the backseat, he knew the setup was a hit.

Between athletics and his studies, there was limited time for socializing during the week. But Jenkins was pleased at how the freshman team was performing in football. Holy Cross had narrowly lost its first game to Dartmouth, to a squad that would go on to become the backbone of an undefeated 1970 varsity team. Psychologically, though, Boston College was the team for Holy Cross to beat. BC was getting a lot of

Eddie Jenkins in his football uniform

Jenkins (left) and Joe Wilson on the practice field

attention for its first-year quarterback, Ed Rideout, and Golden, the freshman coach, decided that he needed to put Jenkins in a better position to score touchdowns. He switched Jenkins from wide receiver to running back for the game.

During the first half of the game, Jenkins got hold of the ball almost two dozen times. He could feel that he was on fire, and the knowledge made him noticeably bolder than usual in the eyes of his teammates. Then, in the third quarter, Jenkins took a serious hit. After having his torso taped to alleviate the pain, he insisted on going back onto the field. "If you carry the ball," said Golden, "you can win the game." Within minutes he scored a touchdown. He had gained 145 yards rushing, a yard less than the entire BC squad. Holy Cross won the game. Jenkins's teammates surrounded him, and the Holy Cross fans yelled with excitement, but the pain in his side was so intense that he felt like screaming as he made his way to the locker room. Jenkins later discovered that he had broken three ribs.

Jenkins first met Father Brooks through football. Brooks had been chatting in Golden's office early in the season when Jenkins came in to see the coach. Golden introduced the priest as the man "responsible for most of you guys being here." The comment struck Jenkins as odd, since it was Golden who had sat in his parents' kitchen and convinced them of the merits of Holy Cross. Golden had shared Brooks's interest in recruiting more black students; the two men had spoken about the need to open up Holy Cross, and Golden had felt encouraged by Brooks's support as he went on recruitment trips. Jenkins shook the priest's hand and cracked a few jokes. Brooks warmed to the freshman player's good-natured sense of humor right away. Nothing seemed to get Eddie down. And as he came to know him better, he came to admire Jenkins's positive attitude and the energy he seemed to bring with him into every room. What came out of his mouth might not always have the ring of truth to it, but the delivery was typically pitch-perfect. He doubted that many people could resist a request from Eddie Jenkins. For his part Jenkins found Father Brooks to be friendly and a little intimidating; the priest was a respectful listener but also supremely confident in his own views. As Jenkins later observed, "Nobody was going to steamroll this man into doing anything he didn't want to do."

Jenkins came to marvel at how socially attuned and all-knowing Father Brooks seemed to be. He couldn't recall a conversation in which the priest didn't seem to already have a grasp of the topic at hand. But Jenkins also found Brooks to be inscrutable: He had no idea what the hell the college dean was thinking beneath the smile. It was a script that would repeat itself throughout his time at Holy Cross: easy banter or lighthearted negotiations with Brooks that rarely strayed into serious topics. Jenkins knew that the joking tone was ultimately because of him. Brooks himself never seemed to have an agenda; he was simply interested and available if Jenkins wanted to talk. It was up to Jenkins to take advantage of that, and he generally preferred to keep the conversation on a lighter note. He wasn't in the habit of sharing his problems with white priests. In fact, Jenkins wasn't comfortable in general with the idea of sharing his problems with anyone, except perhaps Ted Wells, Stan Grayson, and a few other close friends. Brooks may have been warmer and friendlier than some others in the administration, but he was still a member of the administration. He was another person to lobby and charm, an authority figure. Still, Jenkins was always cheered by their occasional meetings and enjoyed running into the priest on campus. He liked Brooks, in part because Brooks always seemed genuinely happy to see him.

As the year wore on, Brooks saw signs that Clarence Thomas was coming to terms with his life at Holy Cross. The sophomore had arrived at the college with a stronger work ethic and drive to succeed than most. Among other things, the rigor of the seminary had helped to make the academic transition a seamless one. Thomas had settled on a major in English, less because of a love of literature than because of his dislike of the Gullah that still occasionally crept into his speech. Other kids had made fun of it in high school, and he knew that any sign of the dialect would prompt people to label him as poor and uneducated. As Thomas later explained, "I didn't want it to define me."

Brooks found it heartening to spot Clarence dashing off to the library and was impressed with his solid grades. But he was even happier to see Thomas socializing with other students, both black and white. For all his inner turmoil, Thomas seemed to be making some good friends. While Brooks noted, with concern, that some of the black students associated almost exclusively with other black men, that wasn't the case with Thomas. The sophomore seemed to get along with practically everyone.

In a private meeting with Brooks, though, Thomas presented a different demeanor. Nothing sat lightly on Thomas's shoulders, whether it was the personal trials of school, work, and family, or the broader issues of race, war, and religion. Like Jenkins, Thomas had found himself drawn to the priest's open nature and clear interest in him. Unlike the freshman football player, though, Thomas was more willing to take advantage of that interest. He needed someone to talk with, and he sensed that Father Brooks was there to listen, not judge. The priest rarely jumped to give advice, unless asked. There were certain truths that he knew—the importance of hard work, the injustice of racism, the need for everyone to feel part of a community—but there were also realities that Brooks couldn't claim to understand. He didn't know what Thomas was experiencing as a black student on campus. Sometimes the sophomore seemed remarkably at ease, and yet he was clearly carrying a heavy load as well.

Moreover, some questions had no easy answers. Thomas was especially worried about the escalation of the war in Vietnam and its potential to derail his ambitions. He didn't trust that a black man could avoid the draft, and Brooks couldn't offer much comfort. It was a common fear on campus. By the end of 1968, American troop strength had reached 540,000. More than 14,000 U.S. soldiers were dead. There was talk that the government was becoming less inclined to let young men sit out the war by staying in college.

Brooks shared Thomas's qualms about the United States sending people to fight a civil war on the other side of the world. While most Americans were not yet aware of the most brutal atrocities of the war, disturbing images were coming across the nation's TV screens every night. The cost of war, an estimated $66 million a day, had forced President Lyndon Johnson to raise taxes and cut back on efforts to reduce poverty, which hurt his popularity and fueled greater opposition to the war. Thousands of young men were being conscripted to fight against their will, and it was clear that more were needed. As a young man, Brooks had been scared to go off to World War II. But at least that was a war his generation understood: Japan had attacked the United States, Hitler and Mussolini seemed determined to control all of Europe, and innocent people were being rounded up into concentration camps to die. The physical and moral perils of doing nothing were obvious then. Vietnam was another matter.

Thomas was determined to do anything to avoid the war. He was afraid of having his career delayed by the draft and of dying in the jungles of Asia. Although he continued to toy with the idea of a career in journalism, he had already told some of the other BSU members that he might study law at Harvard or Yale—he told them he didn't see much point in aiming any lower. Whatever doubts he was having about the rest of the world, he didn't seem to harbor any about himself.

Although his first priority was his grades, Thomas was starting to develop more interests outside the classroom. He was playing intramural sports, and in the spring he did track and field, becoming part of a long-jump team that won a victory over a strong Yale team. He wrote articles for *The Crusader*. He had become a more vocal presence in the BSU, which contrasted sharply with his demeanor in classes, where other students noticed that he often sat in the back and barely said a word. One student suspected it was out of embarrassment about the way he spoke; another felt that Thomas was more interested in learning the lessons than in discussing them—at least in a classroom setting. With so much on his plate, Thomas often felt that just sitting through a class even without taking part in it was all he could manage. He was working about five hours a day in Kimball, trying to catch up on his reading between setting tables, bringing out platters of food, and cleaning up after the other students. But at least he had been quickly promoted to a managerial position at the dining hall, which gave him a small ego boost and a bit more money. As Thomas recalls, he typically got up at 5 A.M. each day to study and spent most evenings, after work and classes, in the library. But even as he pushed himself around the clock, he discovered that college life was becoming more enjoyable than anything he'd ever experienced in Missouri.

Ted Wells wasn't that interested in having a social life, even if his shift in status stung somewhat. His priority was getting his grades up. He spent more time huddled over a desk in the basement stacks of the library on weekends than crammed in the station wagon in search of a party. Although he had been to a few parties with Eddie Jenkins and Stan Grayson, he wasn't eager to meet new women. Within weeks of their formal split, he had reconnected with Nina Mitchell, his high school girlfriend who was studying in Cincinnati. He first wrote her a casual letter, telling her about campus life and the other men he'd met, and she had responded immediately. Soon they were talking on the phone almost every night. The phone bills were so high that Wells had to ask his mother for help covering them. Mitchell had an easygoing personality and loved to laugh, and she was just as ambitious as Wells. The message of the women's movement and black power spoke to her: She shared Wells's passion for learning and intended to get her own degree to pursue a career. By Thanksgiving Ted and Nina had started dating again, and the challenge now was to find ways to see each other. Wells could afford neither the time nor the cost of traveling to Cincinnati.

During one party at Wellesley, Wells told a woman from Newton College of the dilemma he and Nina faced, and the woman suggested that Nina look into transferring to Newton. He immediately asked someone for a piece of paper and scribbled Nina's address on it so that the woman could send her information. It was the first time anyone had seen him ask for a woman's phone number at a party, and they soon discovered why. He had a feeling that Nina would be willing to relocate. Three more years was too long to be apart.

The pressures of football were wearing on Wells. While his transition from playing center to defensive lineman was easy, football felt like a full-time job. He felt torn between the need to study harder and the need to constantly train. Something had to give. He suspected he could become one of the top academic students at the college if he applied himself. The one thing that was standing in the way was football.

Then, on December 11, his mentor, Tom Boisture, suddenly resigned "for personal reasons" less than two years after taking the job. Some players heard there had been a dispute over the varsity preseason training that had taken place in Canada, which might have violated some NCAA rules. Others cited Boisture's poor 3-6-1 record. Among other things, Boisture had started ten sophomores, the youngest players on the varsity team, arguing that they were more talented than some older players. The decision had ruined the already fragile morale of the team. But Boisture's eye for talent later helped the New York Giants win two Super Bowls.

With the coach gone there was even less of a reason for Wells to stay on the team. Still, although he was finding it tough to balance the demands of being an economics major and football practices, he was worried about losing his athletic scholarship; he wouldn't be able to continue at Holy Cross without the money. Shortly after the Christmas holidays, he went to see Father Brooks to ask if he would lose his scholarship if he quit the team. It was a far more personal discussion than they'd previously had when discussing BSU matters. Brooks immediately assured him that the money he received wasn't tied to playing sports. Wells had been admitted on his academic record, too, and his main purpose in coming to Holy Cross was to get a degree. If anyone had issues with Wells quitting the team, Brooks stressed, he would handle them. Wells felt an immediate sense of relief.

While Wells had become friendly with a number of the men on the

team and in his residence, he felt most at home at meetings of the BSU.
He felt closest to Eddie Jenkins, who made him laugh, but who also let
down his guard to show a more thoughtful and serious side when the
two of them were together. Wells had also become good friends with
Stan Grayson, who rarely had a bad word to say about anyone and
seemed willing to take life as it came. The person who needled him a bit
was Clarence Thomas, but Wells enjoyed sparring with him. Whatever
differences they might have had, they both felt passionate about civil
rights, the war, and their own desire to succeed.

The most difficult hurdle to overcome was homesickness. It helped
when Ma Wells would box up large quantities of food like fried chicken,
collard greens, potato salad, chitlins, and cakes, and send them up to
Worcester on the Trailways bus for her son to pick up and share with his
friends. Ted sometimes brought his friends down to Washington for
holidays or the occasional protest march. But little could alter the fact
that he and many of his friends were finding little to like about Worcester itself.

Ed Jones wanted a girlfriend. Even when he did attend some social event,
he found it hard to strike up conversations with women. Most often he
would stand in a corner sipping wine while watching the other men
make their moves. He admired Jenkins for his smoothness. Eddie always
seemed to be talking about different women and heading out to meet
one of them, but Jenkins wasn't the kind of person Jones could go to for
advice. He was too confident, even cavalier, and sometimes he struck
Jones as superficial.

Jones found Stan Grayson more approachable. Of all the men, Grayson seemed to get the most letters from women back home. Jones liked
the idea of writing to someone and having a chance to get to know her
on paper, without the pressure of polite chitchat. He also knew that he
came across better in print than in person. He asked Grayson if he might
consider setting him up with a pen pal. It was an odd request, but Grayson was touched by it. While some of the men might have scribbled

notes to their girlfriends or parents now and then, pen pals weren't supposed to be part of college life. Grayson gave him the name and address of a girl he knew who was living in a suburb of Detroit. Jones wrote her a polite, chatty letter—friendly, he thought, but not too intense. She never wrote back. Jones didn't mention it to Grayson and he never asked if Grayson knew someone else he could contact. He wasn't even sure if the woman had received his letter.

In a June 2011 essay in *The New Yorker*, Jones recalled a letter-writing campaign he'd launched with a young woman he'd gone to high school with in Washington. While he had never kissed her or even touched the back of her hand, he wrote, "I cared for her, and the only way I knew how to express what I felt at that point in my life was to write letters." Unlike Grayson's contact, this young woman did respond to the voluminous correspondence from Jones, if only with what he describes as crumbs about her life. But the mere act of unloading his thoughts and feelings on a remote figure he'd probably never see again was a comfort in the wilderness of Worcester.

The overall experience of being at Holy Cross left Jones cold. Had he gone to Father Brooks's office to discuss it, he wouldn't have known what to say. It didn't occur to him that anyone would want to hear his complaints, and he couldn't think of any way to resolve them. Jones thought a few times of transferring but then dismissed the idea. He wasn't sure where he would go, or who would take him. Instead he switched his major from math to English, where he found more satisfaction, not to mention a way to express his alienation and uncertainty through his writing.

Ed Jones found the social world of Holy Cross stifling. He felt enveloped by his blackness, as though his skin color were always broadcasting itself. Despite the rhetoric about tolerance on campus, he witnessed interactions that made him wonder if the black students' presence at the school was helping to combat racism or making it worse. He heard a student respond, when solicited for the scholarship fund, "tell the niggers to do their own begging." The student then shouted the epithet "nigger lover" as the fund-raiser walked away. The Black Student Union couldn't possibly provide a refuge from that kind of environment. Like Ted Wells, Jones had grown up in all-black neighborhoods. While Jones's experience was far different from that of the high school football star, growing up he had never had to face the kind of blatant intolerance that he felt at Holy Cross. Some of the other black students didn't seem to notice it, or maybe they just didn't let it affect them, but Jones felt a constant chill.

Jones had found an Eldridge Cleaver poster with the message, ELDRIDGE CLEAVER, WELCOME HERE in a Black Panther newspaper and had taped it to the outside of his door. Cleaver was on the lam at that point and nobody knew where he was. His book *Soul on Ice* had become a bestseller, made famous in part by Cleaver's description of the rape of white women as an "insurrectionary act." To some students the poster was the most powerful statement Jones had made all year. They hadn't realized that their quiet and somewhat sullen hallmate was such a radical. Jones liked that fact: He had put up the poster as much to prod the sensibilities of his classmates as to express himself.

On one windy February morning in 1969, Jones returned to his room to find his poster ripped down. Whoever had done it, he thought, had probably done it to make a point about black power. Jones reported the act, and when Brooks learned of it he took it seriously. Although Brooks didn't support the views of Eldridge Cleaver, he saw no harm in displaying an image of the man. Many students had read *Soul on Ice*, and Jones was hardly alone in his admiration for Cleaver and the Black Panthers. Brooks felt strongly that the students needed to respect one another's political views, especially the views of a minority that hadn't necessarily been made to feel welcome. He wanted a more formal inquiry and a chance for Jones to receive an apology. The school couldn't support any act of vandalism or violation of a student's freedom of expression.

A white student down the hall eventually admitted to tearing the poster down and claimed that he had been drunk at the time, though he added that even if he hadn't been he would have torn it down. The student said his roommate had goaded him because four blacks had jumped him a few years earlier. The House Judicial Board ruled that the student had to replace the poster. He never did. With Brooks's encouragement, the board also told the student and his roommate to set up a conference on race relations. Only thirteen of the 140 students in the house came. Jones and the defiant vandal sat down with psychology professor Paul Rosenkrantz to hash things out. But the whole exercise seemed futile and hopeless to Jones. After the discussion, the perpetrators didn't speak to Jones again for months. He felt piercing, condemning looks from others in the hall, as if he himself was the one at fault for having made an issue of the situation.

Other students came to Brooks over incidents of racism. One complained that a carload of white students had tried to run him down—or at least scare him—as he was walking on campus. Another mentioned that white students often got up from dining tables when a black student sat down, or walked out of rooms when black students walked in. Brooks knew the black students genuinely felt racism on campus, but he wasn't convinced that their white classmates were always aware of their offenses. As he later told the *Worcester Evening Gazette*, "White racism is to the white man as original sin is to mankind."

With two dozen black students on campus and efforts to recruit many more for the class of 1973, Brooks wanted to promote more open debate about the state of racial relations at Holy Cross. He was also determined to help raise the profile of campus leaders like Art Martin, who was president of the BSU. He invited Martin, along with other student leaders, to a black-tie dinner for the President's Council, a committee that had been established by President Raymond Swords in 1967 to honor alumni who pledged significant gifts to the college each year. Martin immediately accepted. It meant getting a free seat at the exclusive affair and taking part in a panel discussion the next day, where he planned to raise some of the BSU's issues.

That Friday Martin wore a rented tuxedo, and the men at the dinner, many of them older, treated him as one of their own, as if he were just another promising student attending Holy Cross. He enjoyed the dinner and the experience of being among those with money and power. The next day, however, he showed up on the panel in a dashiki and sandals. He stood and addressed the crowd. "Last night, you didn't see me," he began. "You didn't see me because I was in a suit and tie. I blended in." Some of the alumni shifted uncomfortably as Martin continued. "But now I'm up here in a dashiki, and you notice me. You see I'm different. You see a black man."

Brooks was amused by the proceedings. One man stood up in the room and said that he had sent his son to Holy Cross because he wanted the young man to have a Catholic education, and a good Christian life that would end with him going to heaven. Holy Cross was supposed to be the place, the man argued, where his son would get a moral education and avoid dealing with hippies, protesters, and the ugliness that was happening on the streets. Martin told the man to forget about his son getting into heaven. His kid needed exposure to the real world, and hiding from it wouldn't get anyone into heaven. Martin felt strong and confident as he spoke. He sensed that the world was changing faster than many of the alumni in the room could bear. Even so, when he finished, a number of people in the room applauded.

Brooks often heard similar fears from alumni who came to him in private, sometimes with less civility. One man accused him of risking the school's reputation on a foolish experiment. "I think our reputation is more at risk if we do nothing, don't you?" Brooks had replied. He was in a difficult position. Holy Cross needed the alumni's financial and moral support, especially at a time when the school's finances were so strained—in part because of the generous scholarships Brooks had given out. But Brooks wanted the alumni and the school's trustees to understand the realities of the world. Many of them did, of course: It was hard to escape the revolution. But far too many insisted that Holy Cross remain a refuge, a place where their sons could experience the kind of tough but comfortable education they had received as young men. If black men wanted to enroll, they argued, they were welcome to apply like anyone else; there was no need to seek them out.

Many of the black students were more interested in figuring out how they could escape the real world of Holy Cross than in defending their right to be there. Several of them wanted to establish a "black corridor" where they could live together. They were tired of feeling like they were under surveillance, and the fastest way to get the sense of community they craved would be to create their own physical community.

When the idea had come up at one of the first BSU meetings, Clarence Thomas was immediately opposed. He felt that the plan was equivalent to signing up for segregation. "We fought hard to get into places like this and now we want to segregate ourselves? That's plain stupid," he argued. "We don't need Jim Crow anymore. We're just doing it to ourselves." Thomas knew the rest of the world wasn't going to accommodate whatever needs the black students thought they had. At some point they would all have to deal with the world, and the world would have to deal with them. Thomas was fighting to make it in the world, not just in the black world. What kind of message would the black students send, he argued, if they just shut themselves off from the rest of the college?

Stan Grayson initially leaned toward Thomas's view that integration was best. Like Thomas, he had a number of white friends. And unlike many of the others, he was used to being a highly visible minority from his days at Detroit's All Saints High School. He had coped in that environment and he could cope at Holy Cross, too. He was getting along fine with his white roommate, and he liked the other players on the basketball team. He was also friendly with other athletes, as well as with a number of white classmates from Detroit. In fact, as far as anyone on campus could see, Grayson appeared to have no complaints with the status quo. He was friendly and easygoing with everyone he met.

But though Grayson was used to the occasional ignorant and racist comment from high school, it sometimes still shocked him to hear it at Holy Cross. Some of the other students implied that he wouldn't have been admitted to Holy Cross without his basketball scholarship. They occasionally made snide remarks about the riots in Detroit, mocking "the revolution." The digs didn't happen that often, and they were some-times said in jest, but the message was clear: Grayson should feel grateful that Holy Cross had allowed him to enroll.

In fact, Grayson was worried about his ability to keep up. Along with his major, economics, he was taking English and the required philoso-phy and theology courses. When he wasn't at practice, he was at the li-brary studying, but he still ended the first semester of his freshman year with an embarrassing 2.1 grade point average. The problem was that he had never learned how to study. He went to the library, feverishly read everything, and was overwhelmed by the amount of information he found. He hadn't learned to be strategic, to learn only what he needed to know. He realized that he needed to be smarter about what and how he studied.

But Grayson's concerns over his academic performance and misgiv-ings about creating a black corridor were now taking a backseat. He knew having the black students living together probably wouldn't help the cause of racial harmony, but he was under so much academic pres-sure and felt it would be nice to live in a residence where he could listen to his own music, chat with the brothers, and relax. He had become close friends with Ted Wells and Eddie Jenkins and enjoyed the BSU's Sunday meetings. They were the one time he felt he could kick back and be himself. As he found himself spending more time with the other black students, the thought of living as a group became increasingly ap-pealing.

During their discussions about the dorm, Wells pointed out that they weren't the only black college students calling for some form of community. Across the country, a number of groups were setting up black-only unions and residences. At the University of Michigan, the black students had even established their own table in the dining room. It wasn't segregation, Wells argued. It was sanctuary.

When the final vote for the corridor came up at a BSU meeting, all members were in favor, with one exception: Clarence Thomas. While some of the other men had expressed hesitation over the idea, they didn't feel strongly enough to oppose it. But although the vote was all but unanimous, it created a chasm in the BSU. Some members hadn't shown up for the vote. Others who weren't comfortable with the idea began to drift away from the union.

Nobody was surprised that Thomas's was the sole dissenting vote. Being the dissenter had become a role he assumed at many of their meetings. Once, Thomas decided to defend Booker T. Washington, a former slave and African American leader who had promoted education for blacks around the turn of the century. Some of the other men thought Thomas was incapable of shutting up at BSU meetings, and they found it ironic that he chose to defend Washington for not speaking out against the indignities of forced segregation. W.E.B. Du Bois, a fellow activist at the time, had scornfully labeled Washington "The Great Accommodator" and in 1968, many young blacks were inclined to agree. But Thomas saw Washington as someone forced to do what was necessary to survive. Like Thomas, Washington believed in self-reliance and hard work. He knew the value of getting support from whites. "He was misunderstood," Thomas had said, to hoots of derision from fellow BSU members. Sometimes the opposition was lighthearted, but it could also be heated and verge on real anger. Thomas became used to standing alone.

For his part, Father Brooks was passionately opposed to the idea of the black corridor when Ted Wells and Art Martin first presented it to him. He thought it idiotic and self-destructive. They were raging against apartheid in South Africa and discrimination against blacks in America, yet the students wanted to bring a form of it on themselves. If they wanted to be surrounded by people who looked like them, they should have enrolled at a black college, Brooks thought. Holy Cross was supposed to be a different experience. Everyone found college life unsettling—black, white, rich, poor; it was part of growing up. Brooks had been looking for ways to build bridges and integrate the black students, not the opposite. Nonetheless, he was torn. While he vehemently disagreed with their decision, he nevertheless didn't think it was solely his decision to make. And as much as Brooks was against the notion of black-only housing, he understood the students' reasoning. He knew that many of them were finding the adjustment to Holy Cross harder than they had expected. If the corridor experiment failed, they would only have themselves to blame. If it worked, it might help them achieve the level of comfort that was so far proving elusive.

Brooks suspected that Raymond Swords wouldn't be quite as understanding on the issue. In fact, the president was even more opposed than Brooks. Despite his misgivings, Brooks lobbied the president and the other administrators on behalf of the BSU. At this point, he felt, what mattered was alleviating whatever strains the BSU members were feeling. They had been recruited to get an education, not to prove a point. Brooks didn't think anyone should expect the young men to put their own needs aside in the interest of greater integration. The black students did that every day in their classes. While Wells and Martin liked to talk about empowerment, Brooks understood that what the men really wanted was more comfort, a place where they felt free to be themselves.

The decision to grant the students a corridor set off an inevitable bout of soul-searching and editorials in the student newspaper that questioned both the BSU's request for such housing and the administration's willingness to provide it. Brooks again came out in support of the decision, repeating the arguments he had made to the president. He hoped that the college's efforts to bring in more black recruits in the future might alleviate the need for a black corridor, and he took comfort in the fact that the corridor couldn't be limited to black students alone—there simply weren't enough of them to fill the entire hall. A handful of white students—from the men's existing roommates to others who liked the concept of living with a black majority—had asked to move onto the corridor, too.

A mood of anticipation began to permeate the BSU meetings. Just the idea of having a shared space created a stronger sense of community, and they felt a sense of victory at having achieved their goal. Still, despite the promise of a corridor, some of the recruits simply didn't want to stay on at Holy Cross. It wasn't just the pressure to succeed academically; some of the brightest men were finding it hard to resist the distractions of campus life. What was going on outside the classroom—the parties, protests, and drugs—was far more compelling for many students, black and white, than their coursework. Brooks had tried to reach out to all of the black men in the class of 1972, but some of them weren't interested in speaking with a middle-aged priest. Brooks didn't know who was not planning to come back for the fall of 1969, or who was wavering but might still be convinced. The timing and circumstances around each exit became anecdotal—the student who just stopped coming to class, the one who decided he'd prefer to be closer to home, the one who'd tried and failed to live up to the expectations that Brooks had placed on him. While Brooks could recall the men who came to him when they were having trouble, it was the ones who didn't that would later fill him with angst. He never knew how much some of them were struggling, and he would wonder if he had failed them in some fundamental way.

After he became dean, Brooks found himself dealing with a number of issues in addition to his teaching and religious duties. He was a favorite with many student leaders on campus who found that even if he didn't meet their demands, he would listen and advise. The same was true for students who were struggling with poor grades, a pregnant girlfriend, or any of the other problems that could derail a college education. Brooks was also at the center of discussions about the religious role of the college. With fewer mandatory requirements of students, whether daily Mass or theology courses, the Jesuits were trying to figure out a way to maintain the college's religious identity and values while adapting to the times. They were grappling with how to manage protests against the war overseas while doing more in the war on poverty at home. And while Holy Cross's role in the civil rights struggle might have centered on the recruitment of black students, Brooks and his colleagues were also trying to hire black professors and diversify the curriculum, not because the BSU wanted it but because it was right. What he could do, Brooks believed, was help to move the college in the right direction and be available for the black students whenever they wanted to talk. What he couldn't do, he discovered, was succeed with those who had given up, or change the campus overnight.

In April 1969, near the end of the recruits' first year at Holy Cross, an article ran in *The Crusader* examining the situation of blacks on campus. The reporter, a white student, noted that "a degree of suspicion and mutual animosity exists and will probably continue to grow as more blacks enroll." One black student was quoted as saying that "whereas whites are frankly bigoted in the South, whites here express tolerance, but on the condition that we behave ourselves." A civil rights demonstration across town at Clark University had sparked a typical reaction, the student said: "We were accosted by our white friends and asked why we were making trouble."

Despite such tensions, many of the black men felt they were starting to find a home on campus after the second semester drew to a close. Ted Wells greatly improved his academic performance after withdrawing from the football team, and he was relieved when Nina was accepted at Newton College. Ed Jones began to find solace and a new voice through writing. Maintaining a balance between academics and basketball had proved difficult for Stan Grayson, but his team had had a promising year, and many students thought the school might revive its standing in basketball.

Eddie Jenkins had carved out a reputation for himself on campus. He was likable in many ways, but he also had a dose of bold swagger that some people found hard to take. After contemplating a transfer to the University of Tulsa so he could play for the ousted Tom Boisture, he decided to commit himself to football at Holy Cross. It wasn't so bad, he concluded, especially now that he could live with Wells, Grayson, and the other members of the BSU. He would also be joining the varsity team at a time when people thought the new squad would return Holy Cross to its days of football glory. The press was paying more attention to the team, and he was struck by the surprising number of beautiful black women at neighboring colleges. While he couldn't wait to get back to New York, he knew he'd return to dreary Worcester in the fall, and that was okay.

Clarence Thomas didn't want to go home for the summer. His grandfather had made it clear that he wouldn't be welcome. Thomas tried to convince himself that it didn't matter if his grandfather was supportive or not—he had pretty much written Myers Anderson off as "an ignorant illiterate incapable of understanding or facing the facts about racism." Despite his continued anxieties and self-doubts, he was feeling much more enlightened about the world, especially in comparison to his poorly schooled grandfather. He had made the dean's list and was, in his opinion, now better than the man who had raised him.

Brooks helped Thomas arrange to stay in Worcester for the summer. Through an alumnus, he got him a job at an electroplating company, but the fumes from the plant made him sick and he couldn't keep the job. With nothing to do, Thomas decided to take a trip back home. It was a mistake. He and his grandfather seemed to fight the whole time. As the summer wore on, he vowed never to live at his grandfather's house again.

Across the Northeast, the competition to recruit top black students was building. Although Holy Cross had been the best offer on the table for many of the recruits in the spring of 1968, that was no longer the case a year later. Brooks had handed out more scholarships for the incoming recruits, but he found that the candidates for the class of 1973 had other options and it took more to persuade them to enroll. He thought about what might have happened had the school been recruiting Wells, Thomas, or any of the other men this year. Gil Hardy, for one, had turned down Harvard to come to Holy Cross. Had Hardy waited a year, Brooks had no doubt that Harvard would have sweetened the deal for a smart, black, working-class teen, and Holy Cross would have been left in the dust.

SEVEN

Black Power and a Lost Season

The air was once again crackling with tension when students returned to the Holy Cross campus in the fall of 1969. Over the summer, NASA had put a man on the moon. Any dreams of another Kennedy presidency had been dashed when Mary Jo Kopechne's body was discovered that July in a submerged and overturned car belonging to Ted Kennedy. A Worcester native, Abbie Hoffman, was among the "Chicago Eight" antiwar protesters on trial for disrupting the Democratic National Convention, and police were investigating the gruesome Hollywood murder of pregnant actress Sharon Tate by members of the Charles Manson "family." In August, the Woodstock Music and Art Fair had drawn four hundred thousand people to a dairy farm in upstate New York for a celebration of peace, love, and music. The world was again changing in profound and often uncomfortable ways.

Only a year had passed since the first group of black recruits had arrived and already the campus felt like a different place. A Worcester college consortium had hired an African American professor to teach black literature at Holy Cross and two other schools, and Father Brooks was looking to do much more. Incoming students had been assigned to read *The Autobiography of Malcolm X* and, once again, Eldridge Cleaver's provocative *Soul on Ice* over the summer to sensitize them to the issues and anger of the black community. More important, the total number of black students on campus had grown to sixty-eight, thanks to a concerted recruitment drive. Brooks and his colleagues had traveled to more cities, interviewed more high school students, and given out more money than the year before. While the eighteen freshmen who had arrived in 1968 had received a total of $26,610 a year in scholarships, the forty-one freshmen in 1969 received $105,650 in aid. In a memo to the trustees that August, Brooks argued that although their SAT scores "may not seem impressive in all cases," each of the students had demonstrated leadership skills and had strong recommendations from their schools. He knew that some of the new recruits might not make it at Holy Cross, especially given the difficulties that some of the men had encountered the year before, but Brooks was confident in his ability to spot future leaders. He was looking for men with passion, whether it was a passion for history, writing, or faith in God. What mattered to Brooks was that each student cared deeply about something and had the discipline to pursue that passion. Holy Cross would never move beyond being an institution for the sons of the Catholic elite, Brooks had argued, if it cleaved to tradition at the expense of introducing new thinking.

With their broad range of backgrounds, the black freshmen certainly seemed likely to bring in some new thinking. Brooks and his colleagues had broadened their search beyond conservative Catholic high schools and promising athletes. Holy Cross was now able to attract students who ranged from city kids with Afros and T-shirts to buttoned-up followers of Elijah Muhammad and the Nation of Islam. On the whole, the new group was more radical than the students who had arrived a year earlier, and less interested in whether they would end up in law school than in using college as a way to explore their black identities. Ted Wells and his friends were also becoming more political and less satisfied with the status quo.

There were some tensions among the returning students. Bob DeShay was now living off campus as a senior, trying to have as little to do with Brooks and the BSU as possible. He had already alienated the black athletes with his caustic diatribes about their inflated egos and devotion to sports. "So tell me how running around with that ball is going to save the world, brother," he would say to people like Eddie Jenkins. DeShay now had the black corridor to hate, too. "Congratulations on your resegregation!" he told Ted Wells. Only Clarence Thomas seemed to have a close relationship with DeShay, stemming in part from their shared Georgia background and from the fact that they often agreed with each other on black politics. Notwithstanding Thomas's love of combat gear, neither of them was all that interested in raging against "the Man." DeShay would later recall that he had decided it was more rewarding to hang out with his white hippie friends and smoke pot than deal with the earnest lot now living in the black corridor. "If you're so black and proud, let's have a watermelon party on parents' weekend," he said at one BSU meeting. "We'll celebrate our heritage by sitting on a porch and spitting the seeds out. What do you say? That'll show them how proud black folk like to live."

To outsiders, though, the BSU projected an image of solidarity, and the members all agreed that the bigger the black community, the better. In fact the number of incoming students wasn't as high as the BSU had lobbied for. The previous year, in a meeting with Raymond Swords, Art Martin had told the president that the union expected "no less than fifty" new black students in the incoming class. "If Holy Cross doesn't get these students, the Ivy League will," he stated in an article written by Clarence Thomas for *The Crusader*.

Father Brooks was doing his best to deal with the escalating demands of the BSU. The group had asked Brooks and Swords for a black admissions officer, a transitional-year program to "rectify any inferior secondary school preparation," a black studies curriculum, subscriptions to several black publications in the library, and a special "black meeting and reading room." Swords, incredulous, asked Brooks if he thought they were being serious. Brooks responded that they were. He didn't dismiss the demands as wishful thinking, or as a sign that the young men were becoming too emboldened from getting their way. Brooks saw the list as a clear indication that the students weren't being accommo-

A demonstration at Clark University in fall 1969.
Left to right: Clarence Thomas, Gil Hardy, Ted Wells
(center, in sunglasses), Stan Grayson (second from right).

dated. Holy Cross still had a long way to go if it wanted to become a welcoming place for black students.

Swords didn't like the give-and-take atmosphere that Brooks had encouraged. He felt that the rules and authority of the college were being challenged on a daily basis. He marveled at the audacity of students demanding special concessions in order to feel comfortable. Swords had lived through a war that had affected the lives of a large number of his peers; the world had been changing fast then, too, and he knew that nothing ever moved fast enough for young men. He didn't mind the sense of urgency among the BSU members or among many of the other students on campus. What he disliked was the growing sense of entitlement.

Brooks reminded Swords that most of the black students had never dreamed of attending Holy Cross, because the college had little to entice them. Brooks had convinced these men to come, and the least the college owed them was a few concessions to help them adapt. But Swords was worried about the impact the growing list of perks for a small minority might have on other students or the alumni. A few professors had come to ask Swords whether he thought the black students could handle the workload; they were concerned about letting in more recruits when some of those who had enrolled in 1968 didn't appear to have had the adequate academic training, discipline, ability, or interest to succeed in their studies. Brooks had responded that many of the black recruits were among the top in their class, and that a significant number of white freshmen also struggled and dropped out. The transition to college was rarely easy for anyone. Singling out the difficulties of only black students was fruitless, he argued, and unfair.

The tensions around race had shifted somewhat over the previous year. The anger that had followed King's death had led to some meaningful efforts to address inequalities, at least at the college level. But more black students also meant more demands for teachers who looked like them and courses that reflected their experience. And greater numbers meant less pressure to conform. Before the previous term ended, one senior administrator had written to Brooks and Swords to say that he, for one, was convinced that the college would experience significant problems with the black students within the next year or so. Meanwhile, one sociology professor gave a speech to faculty in which he tried to explain the "totally alien" backgrounds of black students in relation to Holy Cross. "They come from ghetto surroundings; they have gone to ghetto schools, and they have breeded for themselves a ghetto mentality." But some also shared Brooks's view that the onus was more on the faculty than the students to adapt to the times. "The fact is that most of us do not know how to relate to the black students," one Holy Cross education professor argued at an American Association of University Professors meeting. "We have to know something about the heroes and the causes of the black people, just as we know about our own heroes and our own causes."

The mind-set of the black college student was the subject of much discussion, not just at Holy Cross but across the entire country. As more colleges made a concerted effort to admit black students and dealt with the resulting unrest on campus, academics began to study the values and goals of the new black undergraduate population. Black leaders were calling for the creation of a new curriculum aimed at creating a common understanding of black culture. Nathan Hare had been hired to form the first black studies program at San Francisco State University in 1968. He insisted that being black meant you had to be revolutionary and nationalistic. As he wrote in *Newsweek* in 1969, any program "which is not revolutionary and nationalistic is, accordingly, quite irrelevant." Hare lasted only a few months on the job before being fired. Roy Wilkins of the National Association for the Advancement of Colored People (NAACP) believed that segregation—whether in studies or in residences—would likely leave students with a substandard education experience "foisted on them by an administration ready to buy peace at any price."

The debate was fierce on campuses nationwide. Was it fair to subject black students to a body of knowledge that had been forged by centuries of white men? Should race be a factor in admissions? Was any acknowledgment of skin color condescending and, therefore, racist? How much of the burden of racial integration should fall on students? How much should an institution adapt to accommodate black students?

Brooks was skeptical about the many assumptions that intellectuals were making in trying to establish the black students' collective mind-set. As he told one newspaper reporter in Worcester, the "freshmen we brought in measure up in all ways. They are strong personalities and have not folded under some tremendous psychological and social pressures." If some of them came in wanting to be white, he added, that was no longer the case. "They are happy and quite proud they are black and they know they can have a positive effect in a college community."

He fought to get black studies courses into the curriculum that fall, and succeeded in helping to add "Black Literature," "Perspectives on Racism" in the theology department, "Black America" in the history department, and a rather dubiously titled economics course, "The Problem of Blacks and Other Minority Groups." But Brooks refused to draw

sweeping conclusions about race—a game that the black students themselves liked to play. It bothered him that so many people seemed intent
on trying to define who "they" were, as if the experience of being a black
college student could be reduced to one sentence.

Brooks told the trustees that, of the eighteen freshmen who had
come in 1968, sixteen had radically improved their grade point averages
between the fall and spring of their freshman years. One student went
from a near-death 0.8 to 2.5, another from 1.8 to 3.1. He added that
another young man had significantly improved his grades once he received a much-needed pair of eyeglasses.

Brooks suggested that the school do more research on the urban
communities in which many of the black students had grown up. He
argued that the research could be enlightening to all students, remind-
ing the administration that education was supposed to be more than a
path to life in a tree-lined subdivision. The aspirations of each Holy
Cross student were varied, and the curriculum had to become more varied to accommodate them. As Brooks later wrote in *The Crusader*, "Must
we continue to impose on the black man an educational package that is
sealed and designed for those who plan to join the suburbanites?" It
wasn't enough to let in black students, he concluded. The school needed
to change. "Is Holy Cross willing to take the measures necessary to make
up for the deprivations suffered by many black students at the time of
their admission to college?" he wrote. "Unless a genuine and sincere effort is made to remedy these deprivations, there is no social advantage
to be found in admitting scores of black students and then exposing
them to insensitive and possibly resentful professors who demand an
academic performance comparable to that demanded of the more priv-
ileged students."

Brooks placed priority on bringing in black faculty. He reached out
to several academics, including Ogretta McNeil, whom he had met a few
years earlier while she was doing a Ph.D. in experimental psychology at
Clark University. Although McNeil was teaching at nearby Assumption
College, she had done her best to make the black students at Holy Cross
feel welcome in Worcester by inviting them over for dinner parties at her

home. McNeil remembered how lonely it had been for her as a single black mother with two little boys moving to Worcester from New Jersey in 1964. She knew that it would be just as bad, if not worse, for the college students. She admired what Brooks was trying to do at Holy Cross, and had met with him to talk about recruitment. In 1969 they began talking about whether she would be willing to teach at the college, too. The following year she came to Holy Cross as a visiting professor, and she joined the faculty full-time in 1971.

Brooks had come to firmly believe that simply opening the doors of Holy Cross was no longer sufficient. He began calling for "affirmative action"—a term that had first come into official use in 1961, when President John F. Kennedy signed Executive Order 10925. Kennedy had initially wanted job applicants to be treated the same, without regard to their race, creed, color, or national origin. Over the course of the decade, though, the debate had shifted from the desire to be color-blind to a growing belief that equality could only be possible if society addressed the obstacles that were holding some groups back, and acknowledged the advantages that had pushed others forward. That discussion helped to set in place the argument, which Brooks embraced, that characteristics like race should be given extra consideration in any decision—that, all things being equal, the decision should rule in favor of the group that had traditionally had fewer advantages and been underrepresented.

Brooks wanted Holy Cross to go beyond that and acknowledge that black students rarely had the same advantages as the white students in terms of schools, access to resources, or even time to study. Instead of failing black students who struggled, Brooks argued, the college should work with them to help them succeed. His stance was controversial among some of his colleagues, who thought it undermined his earlier insistence that Holy Cross was admitting the same caliber of students, black and white. But Brooks wanted the students to receive extra consideration, not lower standards. Although Holy Cross may have accepted more than three dozen black applicants for the fall of 1969, he made it clear that he had also turned several away. In one letter to an aspiring recruit, Brooks wrote that "in all fairness and justice to you, it must be

said that your chances of succeeding at Holy Cross are impossible, inso-
far as one can reasonably judge, due to the lack of adequate academic
preparation and background." He suggested that the teen go to a junior
college for two years and then apply for a transfer to Holy Cross if his
grades were sufficiently high.

President Swords's views on the subject of race had also developed,
being shaped in part by his many discussions with Brooks. In a commencement address at Suffolk University, he spoke out against what he
saw as modern-day segregation. "A black man lives in an old and de-
crepit city in housing barely within his means, surrounded by white
suburbs with two-acre minimum zoning or other equally effective de-
vices to exclude the disadvantaged." Swords argued that "unless we are
willing to adopt a policy of dispersal of blacks into our white suburbs,
the drift toward apartheid and racial trouble will continue."

As race became a more common topic of discussion on campus, students seemed to become both easily offended and quick to offend. While
students were complaining about "the Man" and "the Establishment,"
alumni were approaching Brooks with their concerns about the "Negro
agenda" and how it might affect the school. The black students began to
take offense at the word *Negro,* a term that a growing number of activists
felt carried the stigma of slavery and oppression. Some white students
asked Brooks why such a small percentage of the student population
was getting such an outsized share of attention. As one young man later
recalled, the dean told him that what benefited the black students would
ultimately benefit every student at Holy Cross, from broader courses to
a richer mix of experiences, and that whatever lifted and unified the
black community would benefit the country.

That was a little harder to see with the black corridor. The Inter-House
Council, which oversaw residential matters, had designated the corridor
as an "experiment," issuing a statement to say that it would likely offer
"opportunity for an increased social life and a more relevant atmosphere for social activity which the white student might take for granted."
Privately Brooks feared the new corridor would in fact ostracize black
students from a wider campus community, although he still stood firmly

by his decision. It could be, and was, portrayed as yet another special perk for the blacks—a sign that they didn't particularly want to mix with their classmates. And that impression wasn't entirely unfounded. One unnamed black student summed up the sentiments of some of his hallmates in a yearbook note, stating that the black corridor "mitigated the devastating effect of the alienation which not only affected our academic lives, but our entire metaphysical being."

The black students returning for their second year at Holy Cross were struck by the change in the campus atmosphere. Stan Grayson marveled at the number of black faces on campus. He felt a little less like an oddity, a little less noticed as he walked around. Furthermore, he was anticipating a good basketball season: He was going to be among the starting five on the varsity team. The year before, the Crusaders had been on a hot streak under Coach Donohue, defeating teams like Syracuse and Georgetown. But the team also had a tendency to choke as the stakes rose. By the final weeks of the 1968–69 season, the team had racked up a strong record of 16 wins and 5 losses—only to lose three consecutive home games and their spot in the playoffs. Grayson hoped he could change their luck this year.

Grayson was also excited to be moving in with his friends on the corridor, including his white roommate from first year, Tom Fulham. Eddie Jenkins and Ted Wells were rooming together, while Ed Jones was living with Gil Hardy. Clarence Thomas, after all his opposition to the idea of a black corridor, had decided to join them and was across the hall with his white roommate from the previous year, John Siraco. There were ten white students living in the new residence. Art Martin, along with his white track co-captain Nicholas E. Ryan, Jr., were assigned to be resident assistants on the corridor.

Some of the BSU members ribbed Thomas about his move onto the corridor, given his earlier protests. He justified his decision by saying that it was important to show solidarity within the group. Even so, a handful of black students had chosen to live somewhere else. One junior, Malcolm Joseph, was viscerally repelled by the idea of living in a black residence. His father had fought in a segregated army unit during

World War II and had talked often about feeling like a second-class citizen. Joseph was happy to be back on campus, having almost quit the year before because of a lack of funds, only to have Brooks find a way to put him on a full scholarship for the remainder of his time at Holy Cross.

For Brooks, one of the biggest highlights of the fall was the start of football season. He was among the growing number of faculty who were raising questions about the cost of maintaining Holy Cross's football program—the view was even shared by some students—but he rarely missed a home game. He had come of age at a time when the franchise was a source of pride. As an undergraduate in 1942, Brooks had seen Holy Cross demolish undefeated Boston College in a 55–12 upset, and he looked back on that season with nostalgia.

The Holy Cross team's recent record was abysmal, which had not helped the team gain support from an administration looking to trim costs. In the fall of 1969, though, everyone was feeling hopeful. Coach Bill Whitton had replaced Boisture, and the players who had circulated a petition the previous year to protest the way the team was being run had come back to school with a renewed sense of purpose. They were determined to improve on the embarrassing record of the 1968–69 season, which had ended with 3 victories, 6 losses, and 1 tie. There was excitement about the newcomers to the varsity team: *Crossroads* alumni magazine described Eddie Jenkins as having the potential to develop into "one of HC's best [running] backs of all time." Prospects looked bright for a winning season, led by co-captains Bill Moncevicz and Tom Lamb. Moncevicz, an offensive lineman, was determined to make his mark before graduating in the spring; his father, Hipolit Moncevicz, had played on the winning 1935 Crusaders team.

As he had the previous year, Jenkins showed up early to start training on August 28. Despite all the optimism, he knew that some players had expressed concern about whether Whitton was the right man to revive the team's fortunes. Whitton had a sharp wit about him and showed a deep knowledge of the game, but he had been a top assistant at Princeton for fourteen years—a long time to have been relegated to a supportive role. Still, Jenkins was flattered when Whitton recognized his abilities as a ballcarrier and decided to make him the only sophomore in the starting lineup.

As the football season began, national and local media outlets were pondering the possible return of Holy Cross as a power in intercollegiate football. The team was looking especially strong on offense. Then the team's prospects took a drastic turn. Just days before the September 27 season opener against Harvard, a sophomore defensive end, Bob Cooney, developed a fever and aches. Everyone assumed it was some kind of twenty-four-hour bug. That evening Cooney tried to flush out his system with glass after glass of water. By the end of the night he was nauseated and reluctantly checked himself into the Holy Cross infirmary a few hours before the Harvard game.

Meanwhile, the team traveled to Cambridge to face off against the Crimson. Jenkins was in good spirits, but he wasn't feeling as energized as he normally did before games. He had been killing himself in practice lately and working hard to keep up with schoolwork, partly to keep pace with his roommate Ted Wells, so his fatigue felt justified. As the team dressed for the game, the locker room was oddly quiet. Players sat warming up their necks and arms as if they were trying to ward off muscle aches, yet the game had not even started.

The Harvard team was the co-defending champion of the Ivy League, but the Crusaders managed to give them a tough run. By halftime, Harvard had a 7–0 lead on its home turf. Holy Cross was still very much in the game, but the lethargy of the visiting players was obvious. Bill Whitton stood at the edge of the field, looking confused. The Holy Cross team needed work, especially on defense, but the players should have been performing at a higher level. As Whitton later told reporters, "we are not as slow a team as we looked." Harvard won, 13–0.

Jenkins thought he had caught the flu. Meanwhile, in the infirmary, Cooney was getting worse and now had jaundice. When a doctor came to see him on the Monday after the Harvard game, he took one look at the feverish player and diagnosed him with hepatitis. Back on the corridor, Jaffe Dickerson was lying in bed, feeling miserable. The coach had complimented him on his agility and speed, so it was infuriating when he noticed that he wasn't moving as fast as he normally did. When the whites of his eyes began to turn yellow, he knew he was getting sick. By the middle of the week, eight of the players had been admitted to the infirmary.

On October 4, the Crusaders headed off to Hanover, New Hampshire, to play Dartmouth College. Even if Holy Cross had been in top form, the game against Dartmouth would have been a challenge. Brooks felt compelled to travel the two and a half hours to the game; he was worried about the team and wanted to show his support. Whitton brought more players on the bus than usual, in case some of them got sick.

The game began badly. Once the play commenced, the Holy Cross players started to literally drop on the field. Some were knocked down and didn't get up; others just dropped onto all fours and stayed there. Jenkins watched his teammates collapsing on the sidelines or crawling off the field on their hands and knees; several of them were too weak to walk. Jenkins was still standing, as were most of the larger players, but the Holy Cross team was disintegrating around him. One of the Dartmouth players approached Jenkins to ask what was going on with his teammates. Jenkins just shook his head. The final tally was Dartmouth 38, Holy Cross 6. Brooks was amazed that Holy Cross had managed to score at all.

By the time the Crusaders returned to the bus, fourteen players were visibly ill. Even the coaches looked woozy. Back at Holy Cross, everyone on the team was tested for hepatitis. A total of twenty players were seriously sick, and fifty-five others who worked on or around the team seemed likely to develop the disease. Even the team's coaches, managers, and PR rep tested positive. A total of ninety-seven people were in danger of developing infectious hepatitis. Yet not a single student, faculty member, or employee not associated with the team had fallen ill.

Brooks and the athletic director reluctantly agreed that there was no choice: On October 6, Holy Cross announced that it was canceling the football season. The players didn't have the energy to practice, never mind compete in the remaining eight games. Brooks also argued that if the team continued with its season, there was a risk that the bizarre epidemic might spill into the general college population. According to a piece that ran a day later in *The New York Times*, it was only the second time in modern football history that a team had "been forced to cancel its schedule because of misfortune." *The Journal of the American Medical Association* later said that thirty-two members of the Holy Cross varsity team had hepatitis with jaundice while fifty-eight people had contracted the illness without signs of jaundice. Only seven of the team members weren't infected.

On the night that the season was canceled, Brooks went to visit the infirmary, where twenty-three men were recuperating; two others were in a local hospital. As Brooks stood in the hallway speaking to a player, the young man slid down the wall and collapsed on the floor. Others could barely open their eyes and struggled to raise their heads from their pillows as Brooks stopped to check on them. Eddie Jenkins had fallen ill, too, and was quarantined with other players in a dormitory for a few weeks. Jaffe Dickerson was battling one of the worst cases on the team and began to question whether he even wanted to continue playing football at Holy Cross.

The team was moved by the responses from other schools. The players at Sacramento State dedicated their season to the Holy Cross team. They wore the Crusaders' purple jerseys and flew the Holy Cross co-captains out to California for their final game. Other teams, including Boston College, sent the school money to help compensate for lost ticket sales. Brooks encouraged Holy Cross students to show their support by attending the freshman team's four games in Worcester. But without the advantage of regular scrimmages with the varsity players, the freshman team only won a single game that season.

Holy Cross invited public health officials and specialists to campus to investigate the causes of the outbreak but it took almost a year to figure it out. There was a family living in a condemned house near the practice field, in which one adult and four children had been diagnosed with infectious hepatitis. The children liked to use the practice field as a playground, and they sometimes urinated on the field and bathed in the water that accumulated around the faucets.

That alone shouldn't have caused an outbreak, but on August 29, 1969, firefighters had been called to put out a fire in a tenement building in downtown Worcester. When they opened two water hydrants, the water pressure on the football team's practice hill dropped, allowing the hepatitis-infected groundwater to seep into submerged pipes near the field. With the extreme heat the day of the fire, most of the Holy Cross players drank several times from the infected faucets. The coaches also used the water to make "cactus juice"—a mixture of vinegar, minerals, and salt that was similar to the University of Florida's new invention, Gatorade, named after the Gators football team. Everyone who drank water from the hose that Friday afternoon fell ill.

For public health officials, the epidemic was a fascinating and disturbing mystery. For the players, it was a bitter disappointment. As he tried to adjust to the idea of a year without football, the lingering question for Eddie Jenkins was whether it would have a lasting impact on his career. Robbed of an entire season of play, and struggling to recover in the fall of 1969, he wondered if his NFL dreams were now dashed. As a sophomore player, he'd have two more years to prove himself. In the meantime, he now had the time and the incentive to turn his attention to other parts of campus life.

EIGHT

Freedom and War

Throughout the fall of 1969, Father Brooks was struck by the changes in the black students who'd arrived a year before. He knew that most of them were young men on whom a lot of pressure had been placed, often the first in their families to attend college. Having survived a tough freshman year, they now acted in one of two ways: Some had coped with the isolation and stress they felt by turning away from their studies, and others had stepped up their game. Brooks kept a close eye on the students who were falling behind. He solicited feedback from their professors, trying to find time to talk with them on campus or gently pushing the president to invite them to dinner to boost their morale. One black student even recalls the dean encouraging an underperforming roommate to remain active in antiwar protests, even complimenting him for speaking up against a U.S. policy that Brooks agreed was wrong, while also advising the young man that the best way to promote social justice was to become a successful role model for others. "Don't forget why you're here," Brooks had said. The dean also kept note of who appeared to be doing well, not just in class—grades were important but not sufficient to turn young men into leaders, in his view—but in the other aspects of campus life. He was pleased to see that Ed Jones and Clarence Thomas were writing for *The Crusader*, and he thought the entire student body would benefit from the growing vibrancy of the BSU on campus, now led largely by Ted Wells as Art Martin tried to focus on his senior year of study.

Several changes had made the men feel more welcome, from the increased numbers of black students on campus to efforts, however mild, aimed at increasing awareness of the black experience through the curriculum. For the men who had been recruited to Holy Cross the year before, though, the critical difference was the chance to live together on the top floor of Healy Hall. The black corridor was both an oasis and a unifying force for its residents. While Brooks continued to face blistering criticism from some colleagues for having supported a segregated residence, he had grown less bothered by it once he saw the benefits. He sensed that most people on campus now sympathized with the desire of the black students to create a place of their own within Holy Cross. The Jesuits shared a common residence; the black students had a right to forge a closer community. More important, those living on the corridor seemed notably happier about living at Holy Cross. Clarence Thomas was privately relieved about his decision to join the experiment. The fact that his sophomore roommate, John Siraco, and several other white students were also living on the corridor had made it easier to justify moving there himself. Even so, the overall vibe was decidedly black, and that's what Thomas liked. It was, as he put it, comfortable and a place where he felt he belonged. There were pictures of black leaders and symbols of black power on the students' doors. The music drifting into the halls was more Motown than Haight-Ashbury, with Marvin Gaye and the Temptations occasionally battling with Jenkins's Nancy Wilson tunes. For the first time in his memory, Thomas felt he didn't have to explain himself to anyone or live under the watchful eye of other people. He continued to be more focused on his schoolwork than on having fun—the most predictable part of Ed Jones's day soon became seeing Thomas returning home a few minutes after the library had closed at 11 P.M.—but he now found himself connecting with men other than his roommate, standing in the hallway to share a laugh with Gil Hardy or complain about his lack of money.

Thomas's closest bonds were with Hardy and the Georgia boys, especially Al Coleman and Bob DeShay. He was concerned that DeShay, now a senior who was living off campus, seemed to be spending more time socializing than studying. The situation with Al Coleman was even more troubling: A brilliant sophomore who awed the other men with his ability to read a book from start to finish every day, Coleman rarely bothered to go to class and had only managed to squeak through the previous year because he'd performed well on his finals. Gil Hardy, on the other hand, clearly shared Clarence's ambition and drive to succeed, and was among the top-performing students in his class. Thomas found it amusing that people underestimated Hardy because of his Philadelphia slang, and it also comforted him to know that he wasn't the only person who was pegged as less intelligent because of the way he spoke.

Hardy and Thomas also shared a sense of humor, which even some of their hallmates found surprisingly juvenile. They sometimes delighted in the crude, throwing out playful insults and obscenities while sometimes addressing each other as "bitch." Some students reported coming home from dates only to have Thomas persistently press them for details of what had happened in bed. Another recalled being shocked by Thomas's tendency to talk about explicit body parts—his or others—and tell people what to do with them. How these memories may have been shaped by later feelings about Thomas's performance on the Supreme Court or his alleged harassment of Anita Hill is unclear, but Thomas himself admits there were probably times when the jokes went too far. "We were kids," he says now. "I'd gone from wearing a cassock and preparing for the priesthood to being a mixed-up kid at college in the late 1960s." Regardless of his interest in the other men's sex lives, Thomas was not looking to meet women himself. He was still smitten with Kathy Ambush, the Anna Maria College student whom he had met through Jenkins during his sophomore year. He liked that Ambush spoke her mind and had a sharp sense of humor, and he especially liked her family. Unlike his grandfather, her parents never made Clarence feel small or unworthy. Years later Thomas would still recall fondly how

Kathy's father, a technician in a dental lab, made him everything from a workspace in the Ambush home to a bridge that kept his drifting teeth in place. To the men on the corridor, Thomas seemed more confident and happier than they'd ever seen him.

There were times when the overall atmosphere on the corridor was raucous. The men lampooned one another, whether it was teasing Philadelphia recruit Walter Roy for his short stature or Eddie J. for his good looks. The containers of food from Ma Wells to her son arrived frequently, in portions big enough to share with the other men. Weekends brought parties and bottles of Ripple, a cheap fortified wine that was Thomas's particular favorite, as well as beer, malt liquor, and marijuana for the few who partook. They also brought visits from girlfriends like Nina Mitchell, who had transferred to Newton College of the Sacred Heart and would often make the forty-five-minute trip down from Boston to see Ted.

Wellesley had become a favorite for the black students of Holy Cross—in particular, the women of its Ethos Choir. The choir was composed exclusively of African American women who were part of the Ethos black student group. While the choir visited numerous campuses in the Northeast, the reception they got from the black men at Holy Cross was so enthusiastic that the college quickly became a popular stop for the women, too. The BSU members would often meet the choir at their bus with flowers and escort them around campus. Clarence Thomas even composed a poem that he distributed to other men on the corridor, exhorting them to treat all the sisters who came to the college well. The title: "Is you is, or is you ain't, a brother?" A high proportion of trips off campus soon involved a stop at Wellesley to see how the Ethos sisters were doing.

The men on the corridor also had a shared cause in a "Free Breakfast for Children" program that sophomore Lenny Cooper had helped start in Worcester. It was modeled on a program that the Black Panthers had launched in Oakland, California, at the start of 1969 with the goal of feeding inner-city children before they went to school. Although touted as an initiative to help black children, the reality was that Worcester's tiny black population, which stood at about 2 percent of the total, meant that many of the kids being helped were actually white. Nevertheless, it gave the BSU members a chance to get involved in the movement and put their beliefs into action.

The challenge was finding a steady stream of men willing to get up at dawn to head downtown and make breakfast for a bunch of kids. Although Thomas was among the most vocal of the volunteers in the breakfast program, and often gets credit in the media for starting it, Ed Jones was a much more regular participant. Jones didn't mind getting up early. He found that he enjoyed seeing a side of Worcester that was so different from the sometimes stifling atmosphere of the campus. Walking by the manicured lawns and stately buildings of Holy Cross, it was easy to forget that they were living in an industrial city that had seen its share of hardship as manufacturing jobs came and went. Besides Jones and later Lenny Cooper, from the class of '72, the steadiest presence was Gordon Davis. Many mornings, Davis and Jones would go knocking on doors along the corridor at 6 A.M. to see who was available to help out. Thomas tried to go a day or two a week. Al Coleman, the Savannah sophomore who'd cut class to read, also let himself get dragged along, as did Eddie Jenkins because he liked to cook. Most of the others pretended to sleep, or would yell that they had been up late and would be lucky to feed themselves that morning, never mind the hungry children of Worcester.

With so many distractions, it was easy for some of the men to lose sight of why they were at Holy Cross. Not so for Ted Wells and Clarence Thomas. During the week they were more likely to run into each other at the library than on the corridor. Both men were known to put pressure on the other black students to hit the books. More than once, Thomas tried to take Coleman to task for skipping class, saying, "Man, what are you doing? You've got the rest of your life to fool around." Wells's tactics were more playful, but also more frequent. Wells shared Brooks's view that the men who had made it to Holy Cross had an opportunity to make something of themselves and, in fact, had a responsibility to do so. The only way to prove that they deserved a spot at Holy

Cross was to excel once they got there, and the best way for black men to prove themselves equal to whites was to outperform them now that they had finally gotten the chance. Although growing up in a positive all-black environment may have buffered Wells from discrimination, he understood the stereotypes. Their job was to break them. Otherwise the doors that were starting to open might just as easily swing shut again.

While Wells liked to socialize, especially after coming back from an evening of study at the library, he also saw the men's proximity as an opportunity to exert some friendly peer pressure. If he saw someone reading a magazine or listening to music during exam time, several hallmates recalled, he inevitably would speak up: "So you ready for that test, brother? I don't see you studying."

Wells saved his most direct admonitions for Eddie Jenkins, who shared a room with him, except for the weeks he was forced to spend living in quarantine that fall with the rest of the football team. One night, while Jenkins was getting ready to close his books after studying for a political science test, Wells said, "J., what are you doing?"

"Getting some sleep, man," said Jenkins. "It's one in the morning."

"What do you think you'll get on that test?"

"I don't know," Jenkins replied." Maybe a B."

"Man, how can you settle for a B when an A is still on the table?"

"It's not a big deal."

"Man, they're all a big deal. You only get one shot."

Bleary-eyed, Jenkins went back to his desk. He ended up getting an A-minus on the test.

The Black Student Union now held its meetings on the corridor on Sunday nights after dinner. Though the BSU agenda could range from suggestions for social events to complaints about the deteriorating BSU van, a few common themes emerged. Despite the larger numbers, the men seemed even more dissatisfied with the black presence on campus, from the number of students and faculty to the dearth of courses on black literature and history. Holy Cross had not moved fast enough or far enough, in their view. And few BSU meetings would pass without some debate over how to respond to racism, perceived or overt, as well as the turmoil on other campuses and issues on the national scene. Lenny Cooper recalled emotions running high over incidents like a white student loudly complaining about the prospect of "jigaboo broads" coming to campus mixers, which had provoked a fistfight. They argued about the latest edicts from groups like the Nation of Islam, and whether the BSU should issue official statements on university policies or developments in the Vietnam War.

While "Daddy Art" Martin remained the BSU's official chairman, he had opted for a less active role in order to focus on getting into a good law school. Nobody seemed to mind vice chair Ted Wells taking on a bigger leadership role; running the union and lobbying the administration on BSU demands seemed less like a perk than a hassle to most of the men. Wells, though, enjoyed it. He shared his mother's philosophy that the best way to get things done was to win people over and almost embarrass them into being nice. Anger at injustice could be powerful; anger at a fellow brother was a sign of weakness.

That stance helped Wells to handle both the anxieties that everyone felt about the times and the eclectic mix of new students. Several of the freshmen who had arrived that fall were more extreme in their views of racial justice and more willing to consider extreme action. One newcomer invited a Black Panther to speak to the BSU members. Another introduced a motion to buy guns and shoot all the white people, to right the wrongs of slavery. His proposal prompted roars of laughter instead of a vote. Another suggested that, since the food in Kimball was so bad—itself a matter of debate to men like Stan Grayson, who still praised its high quality—the entire BSU should become Muslim and demand a special diet. Wells tried to remain unflappable, always ready with a "yes, brother" or "interesting point, brother" before moving people along to the next item on the agenda.

Although the BSU membership had more than doubled in number, Ted Wells and Clarence Thomas continued to command a hefty share of attention at the BSU meetings. As often as not, the argument would start when Wells presented his thoughts on a given topic on the agenda. Thomas would then speak up to offer an alternate view. The two men would then get locked in a debate. To Grayson, it felt less like Thomas was passionately arguing on principle than that he was simply enjoying the challenge of playing devil's advocate. Thomas liked to dissect an argument and turn the arguer's logic against him, much like a cross-examination. Sometimes Thomas would even end with a laugh, leaving the men unsure of where he actually stood on what he'd just said. And Wells seemed just as pleased to pick apart Thomas's points. The frequency of the clashes between the two men prompted Grayson to start dubbing the BSU meetings "Sunday Night Theater."

On some topics, though, Thomas did feel strongly. He resented the apparent assumption—by both the BSU and by Father Brooks—that every one of the black students needed money, coddling, and special services to make it at Holy Cross. The people who needed help, he argued, were any students who couldn't afford to pay the tuition. The father of one black student from the prosperous Shaker Heights suburb of Cleveland had felt insulted when Holy Cross offered his son aid for the fall of 1969, and he had turned it down. Thomas argued that if the BSU pushed the school to limit scholarships to the students who really needed them, that might free up enough money to allow more black men to enroll. Wells challenged Thomas to find one member who was getting a completely free ride at Holy Cross. Most of the BSU members were waiting tables, taking part in research projects, delivering newspapers, and becoming resident assistants to help make ends meet. They were no better off, in his view, than many white men whose parents were helping them foot the tuition bills. As far as Wells could tell, Holy Cross had so far been unable to attract wealthy black students, and he argued that it had to offer some incentive for black students to spend four years in a cold and somewhat unfriendly environment.

The entertainment value of Thomas's speeches masked the reality that he did feel at odds with many of his hallmates. While the increasingly strident tone of discourse at BSU meetings didn't seem to bother

Wells, it was wearing on Thomas. Despite the comforts and camaraderie of the corridor, Thomas started to feel a greater distance from many of the other black students. He felt there was something narcissistic about their general worldview and it bothered him that they seemed to feel they could cast stones with impunity because they were oppressed. He didn't like the way it was assumed that the black man was inherently without sin. He hadn't felt as out of sync with the other black students a year earlier, when the BSU was much smaller and Wells was his main opponent in debates. Even when they fiercely disagreed, Thomas had assumed that Wells shared his fundamental belief that the best way to take on the Man was to beat him at his own game. Now he wasn't so sure; even Wells seemed to have embraced the idea that the college owed them extra privileges because of their skin color. Thomas wondered how many men in the eclectic class of 1973 would graduate and go on to forge successful careers. Thomas loved Father Brooks, but it bothered him that the dean seemed to bend to whatever the BSU wanted. It felt condescending somehow, like Brooks thought they might not be tough enough to cope with the realities of Holy Cross on their own.

The person Thomas was hardest on, though, was himself. It wasn't just about getting people to look beyond his skin color: Nothing seemed to bother him more than the sense that he might be characterized as average or merely good. One of his old professors remembers the way Thomas would visibly bristle at the notion. None of Thomas's grades went unexamined; even the solid ones prompted a visit from him, asking the professor how he could do better the next time. By his junior year, simply being smart wasn't enough for Thomas; he had to be recognized as being smart. The issue wasn't simply one of pride. After dabbling with the idea of a career in journalism, he now had law school at Harvard or Yale in his sights.

The fun that Thomas seemed to have at many BSU meetings and on the corridor was far from evident in the classroom. There he could come across as serious, industrious, and almost grim in his determination to succeed. While he got high grades for his thorough and straightforward arguments, some of his professors didn't always find him fun to teach. Classmates recall that he rarely spoke or asked questions during discussions, a trait that continued and created some controversy after he was appointed to the Supreme Court. Still, in a 1994 speech, Thomas looked back on his Holy Cross days and talked about the inspiration that he had found in classes like Readings in Renaissance Prose, where he was able to see parallels between his own beliefs and those of historic characters. He became fascinated with the childishness of Wolsley in *The Life and Death of Cardinal Wolsey,* and with the steadfast courage of More in *The Life of Sir Thomas More,* comforting his executioner at his beheading. How much better to be like a Thomas More than like a Cardinal Wolsey, Thomas told his audience, "rising as the wheel rises but then tragically crushed or splattered with mud as it descends." Such heroism not only inspired him, Thomas recalled; it also helped him to crystallize his thinking on the importance of character and morality. It helped him to deal with the hypocrisy he saw around him.

Wells, too, was bothered by the contradictions that he saw on campus. Although people talked about equality, popular opinion seemed to be that most of the black men at Holy Cross were recruited more for their muscles than their minds. Long after Wells dropped out of football, classmates continued to ask him what sport he played. The easygoing temperament that he showed in handling BSU meetings was harder to summon up when reacting to insults in public. In response to a letter in *The Crusader* from a fellow student who called on blacks to "relax and be magnanimous over the wrongs you suffer," Wells wrote that "I knew that if I stayed at Holy Cross long enough, some benevolent White man would show me the right path to follow." He continued with an offer to shine the student's shoes, carry his books, and create a "Black ROTC" to train more brothers to fight in the "White man's wars."

As he settled into his sophomore year, Wells found that his relationship with Father Brooks began to shift. While the two still enjoyed warm conversations on a regular basis, Wells took his enhanced responsibilities in the BSU seriously. He wanted the BSU to take a more active role in black recruitment. To him it didn't make sense to have recruitment directed out of the dean's office. Wells felt that the black students might prove to be better ambassadors in recruiting students than white administrators. But he noticed that Brooks wasn't exactly applauding his ideas: When Wells wrote up a letter to send to black applicants to the class of 1974 advertising Holy Cross's generosity toward its black students, Brooks shot back a curt response to the admissions director. "I suggest you explain to Ted Wells that *he* is not able to *guarantee* financial assistance" (underlining the words *he* and *guarantee* twice). "This is the prerogative of the President." The black students could meet with recruits and show them around, but that was it. Brooks was always willing to listen, though, especially where the students were concerned, and could even be moved to a different point of view after hearing a compelling explanation: Stan Grayson, for one, got his wish to strike the phrase "Old Black Joe" from the lyrics of "Mamie Reilly"; it was replaced with "Go Cross Go." But Wells also understood that whatever friendship existed between him and Brooks, the boundaries were clear: He was the student and Brooks had the power. The dean would listen respectfully and ask questions, but he wasn't going to cede authority. While the times may have spurred a seemingly endless list of requests from the BSU and other student groups, Brooks's priorities when deciding on a response came down to a few simple questions: Was it something that might help the students succeed? Could they afford it? And was it the right thing to do?

Ed Jones was becoming more concerned about issues of social justice during his sophomore year and had started to express his views through a column that he had suggested writing for *The Crusader*. He had bought a typewriter and could be heard clacking away on it at all hours, writing pieces about the hypocrisy of people like black tennis star Arthur Ashe who "have mental miscarriages when they can't play with the doomed whites of South Africa" or golfers like South Africa's Gary Player deigning to "descend their ladders to make money for an American black college fund."

Jones also channeled his discontent into protests; his willingness to go almost anywhere in support of a cause had helped him to strengthen his bonds with hallmates like Gordon Davis and Al Coleman. Every weekend there was a protest of some kind, from small gatherings over labor issues in Worcester to large antiwar marches in other cities. Jones felt invigorated and part of a community, if only for the duration of each march. When other men weren't available to go, Jones began to head off to Clark University alone, where there always seemed to be a bus going to some demonstration. That fall he met a young woman from a neighboring college on a trip to Washington. He took her to his mother's apartment one evening, hoping to surprise his mom with a visit. When they got there, his mother was still at work and his companion suggested that Jones leave a note. "She can't read," Jones had replied. The young woman was struck by how sad he looked as they walked out, leaving his mother with no sign that they'd ever been there.

Jones's forays into the counterculture only went so far. The drug culture held little allure for him. His most direct exposure to marijuana was after a protest in Boston, when he, Coleman, and another student decided to walk the more than forty miles home. As the sun was coming up, a man stopped to offer them a ride and some pot. Jones got into the backseat, watching as the man lit a joint and passed it around. The smell alone had made him a bit nauseated. Drugs would never be his thing. The free love movement didn't affect him, either, and Jones tended to avoid parties. On the few occasions he was dragged to one, he would stand alone, drinking soda or perhaps a beer while watching the others chat up women.

Jones met his first real girlfriend on one of his D.C. bus trips, a quiet white girl who was a commuter student at Anna Maria. Jones liked the fact that she shared his passion for ending the war and promoting civil rights, and he found her very attractive. She wasn't the usual type he saw at demonstrations; she was conservative, in keeping with the mores of her Catholic girls' college. Although she seemed to enjoy his company, their courtship was a tentative one. He never told the men that he was dating someone, never mind a white woman. Moreover, as the year progressed, it felt more like a friendship than a romance.

Stan Grayson had been working hard to raise his game as the basketball season began that fall. He had a wider social circle than most of the men on the corridor, and was spending as much time with white students as with black students; he didn't always sit at the de facto "black table" at Kimball. Grayson wasn't immune to racial tensions; he simply tried to ignore them. But his coach, Jack Donohue, sometimes got to him. An article had recently appeared in *Sports Illustrated* in which Lew Alcindor recalled Donohue, then his high school coach, accusing him of acting "just like a nigger!" The piece had been circulating all over campus.

Donohue had built a reputation for himself as a father figure to inner-city boys. The *Sports Illustrated* piece tarnished that image. It also diminished the pride Holy Cross felt at having hired the coach who had shepherded Alcindor to greatness. But the article hadn't surprised Grayson. Even during his first year on the team, when he figured he was just getting used to a new coach, he saw signs of bias in Donohue.

Donohue had a wonderful wit and was never short on stories for every occasion. But he also seemed to associate certain traits—being late, not putting in the effort—with being black; he referred to the late starting time of games or practices as "Negro time." Grayson found the slang especially insulting because he prided himself on never being late.

Donohue pulled Grayson aside before a game in October to address the accusations in the magazine piece. Despite Donohue's brazen attitude, he was sheepish when he told Grayson that important elements of the article were inaccurate. Donohue was clearly embarrassed when explaining that he had called Alcindor a "nigger" once because the young player was being lazy. "You know what I meant," he said. Grayson wasn't sure how to respond.

"Sure, coach," said Grayson. "I know what you meant." They never spoke of the matter again.

Stan Grayson during a Crusaders game

The team was finding it hard to thrive under the larger-than-life Donohue, and it hadn't performed as well as expected. Grayson certainly didn't think he was playing at the top of his game. At six-foot-four, he was a relatively small man for many positions, but Donohue kept trying to play him as if he were another version of the seven-foot-two Alcindor. Some of the players balked when the coach reacted to their missteps with ridicule, and many got used to hearing Donohue yell, "Who the hell told you this was a democracy?" if challenged on decisions. While Donohue's sharp wit and brusque style kept things lively, some players felt it did little to build their own confidence or the team's morale.

Grayson had been dating a woman from Detroit who was attending the University of Michigan, but the distance was too great and they had split up. On a trip to Washington with Ted Wells, he met Vicki Mitchell, the younger sister of Ted's girlfriend, Nina. Grayson really liked her and discovered to his delight that Vicki was attending Anna Maria College, just outside Worcester. It wasn't often that he met women who lived close to Holy Cross; the options around Worcester were limited, in large part by the men themselves. There was an unspoken rule that black men should date within the black community. When Clarence Thomas once saw a black girl walking with a white man on campus, a hallmate recalled he did an exaggerated double take and joked that the revolution might be going too far. The BSU even staged a mock trial for a black man dating a white woman. When the man was judged guilty, they broke his Afro comb as punishment. It was all meant in jest, but the message to the members was clear. When some BSU members later decided to draft a missive on "the black man's philosophy," dating black women was placed at the top of the list. Rule #1 stated that "the Black man must respect the Black woman. The Black man's woman is the most beautiful of all women." After some other rules that spoke to the black man's superiority and his need for separation, the members went back to the subject of dating with Rule #9: "The Black man does not want or need the white woman. The Black man's history shows that the white woman is the cause of his failure to be the true Black man."

What unified the BSU in 1969, though, was war, not women. While Jaffe Dickerson was recuperating from hepatitis that fall, he learned that his older brother's jaw had been blown off in Vietnam. Eddie Jenkins's brother had called him on a handset from the Khe Sanh combat base and told him that every time he put up radar, it got shot down. Muhammad Ali, who had been convicted of draft evasion, stripped of his heavyweight title, and banned from boxing in 1967 for his refusal to serve in Vietnam, had become a hero after famously stating that "I ain't got no quarrel with them Viet Cong." Free on bail as he appealed his conviction, Ali had been touring colleges around the country to speak out against the war.

At BSU meetings, the impending draft lottery on December 1 was an increasingly emotional issue. President Nixon had promised to end the war in Vietnam and review the Selective Service System in the hope of moving to an all-volunteer army. In the meantime, though, Nixon had signed an amendment to have conscription determined by random selection. It was the first draft lottery since 1942. To address complaints that too many poor black men were sent to serve, there would be no college deferral. Everyone born between 1944 and 1950 would be eligible, with the date of birth used to determine the order that people would be called for induction.

The event, held at the Selective Service headquarters in Washington, D.C., was broadcast via radio and TV. On the corridor everyone gathered to listen to the results. Only one of the black students from the class of '72, Stephen Collins, was too young to make the cut. The others couldn't afford to go to Canada to dodge the draft, nor did they have the contacts to get them into the National Guard. If they were chosen, they would be put on a plane and sent to fight.

Each day of the year was written down on a piece of paper and rolled into plain plastic capsules that were then placed in a large glass container. There were a total of 366 capsules—an extra one for men who had a leap-year birthday. Someone in the corridor put on Marvin Gaye's *What's Going On* as the men gathered together to watch as Congressman

Alexander Pirnie of New York reached in to pull out the first capsule. All the men had put five dollars into a pot. Whoever had their birth date called first would win the jackpot.

The first capsule chosen contained the date September 14. The men were relieved to find that it wasn't anyone's birthday. Nine more capsules were opened and everyone in the corridor cheered as the dates passed by. With each date they could hear whoops and yells from other parts of the building.

Then the voice over the radio read out "August 31," and the room fell silent. That was Eddie Jenkins's birthday. Jenkins had won the jackpot. He tried to laugh but he felt tears welling up in his eyes. He didn't want to die in a jungle somewhere, but with his No. 11 standing, it looked certain that he would have to go.

The cheerful mood was fading fast. Ed Jones was No. 24. He thought of the forced marching he had endured for years in the Washington High School Cadet Corps. Like Ted Wells and other young men from the capitol, Ed Jones went to high school at 7:45 A.M. twice a week to perform one-hour drills in all the military movements—about-face, column left, column right, port arms, right shoulder, left shoulder, parade rest. He knew the military alphabet—Alpha, Bravo, Charlie—and the fact that the M-1 rifle weighed nine and a half pounds. Maybe that would help him in Vietnam.

Clarence Thomas's birthday came up as No. 109, while Stan Grayson was No. 158. Only Ted Wells looked like a long shot at 272.

Anyone whose birthday came up in the first two hundred capsules stood a strong chance of being called to report for duty and would likely find himself assigned to the ground army, where much of the fighting and most of the fatalities took place. Jenkins began to have nightmares, wondering when his letter would arrive.

Brooks understood the students' fears: Although he had volunteered for service, he knew the difference between wanting to fight and being forced to fight. When some of the men with low numbers had come to see Brooks after the lottery, he had felt at a loss as to how to comfort them. There was nothing that he or anyone else at Holy Cross could really do. As long as the United States continued to play a role in the Vietnam conflict, the country would need a steady supply of young men to keep up the fight. All across the campus, a large portion of the student body now had a much more personal reason to protest the war.

NINE

The Walkout

By late 1969, antiwar protests had become an unavoidable part of campus life. While some students took an active role in the ROTC and supported American efforts to defeat North Vietnam's communist forces, a growing number were angry and desperate for the United States to pull out. Opposition to the war was fueled by the rising body count of American dead and reports of the mass murders of hundreds of unarmed Vietnamese women, children, and elderly villagers by U.S. troops in what became known as the My Lai Massacre. Soldiers came home and spoke of abuses; journalists went with their cameras and documented the horrors of the war on film. Nationwide, students were looking for any opportunity to make themselves heard on the war or on any matter of social injustice.

Holy Cross was ripe terrain for anyone looking to protest the war. The college had a long-standing ROTC presence and was a popular recruiting spot for the military as well as companies with military contracts. The steady stream of recruitment visits gave antiwar protesters easy targets for demonstrations. In the fall of 1969, the Holy Cross chapter of Students for a Democratic Society staged a "talkathon" when Marine recruiters came to campus. They chanted so loudly that the officers were unable to interview potential recruits. While tensions were high, most of the demonstrations passed without incident. During a march to protest an insurer's involvement in a controversial urban renewal project, police met the protesters at the company's headquarters in full riot gear with dogs and reinforcements. The police ordered the students back to campus, and they left without any real arguments. None of them wanted to go to jail or get into real trouble.

Brooks firmly believed in the students' right to protest. Occasionally he even joined them. At one October event, a large group of students gathered on the library steps to call for a moratorium on U.S. involvement in Vietnam. Brooks gave a speech in support of the students, and then he and Swords held an impromptu mass for everyone who showed up.

Minor campus confrontations continued throughout the fall of 1969. The SDS morphed into the Revolutionary Students Union (RSU), and the new group devoted much of its effort to going after the ROTC. They argued that the volunteer organization was an especially toxic force in the military machine because it helped to train officers who would then give orders to men who'd been drafted into battle against their will.

On December 1, the faculty senate took a vote to state that, among other things, "advocates of no cause will be permitted to deny freedom to anyone with whom they may disagree." Moreover, when it came to career recruiting, the campus "must remain open to the representatives of business firms and agencies of government which enjoy a legitimate place in American society."

The RSU vowed to continue with its protests in spite of the vote, especially after learning that its threat of a protest had prompted the cancellation of a December 3 visit by the Central Intelligence Agency. Next up was a General Electric Company recruitment visit on December 10. Protesters saw that as an opportunity to log yet another victory. The RSU announced that it planned to interrupt the GE visit in support of an ongoing strike by GE workers and to protest the company's role as a major defense contractor that manufactured products like the Minigun, a helicopter-mounted weapon that could fire up to four thousand rounds per minute.

The RSU organizers approached Ted Wells and Art Martin to see if the Black Student Union wanted to join the protest, since GE had been accused of discriminating against African Americans. Wells was skeptical; he argued that the BSU should save its energy for battles that were more directly related to black issues, but he agreed to take the matter to a vote. The black students met on December 9 and, after some debate, agreed that the union should stay neutral. Anyone who wanted to join the protest would have to go on his own.

The next morning, two GE recruiters arrived on campus. Holy Cross officials met them in the parking lot and took them straight to Room 320 of Hogan Hall. Within half an hour, a few dozen students had gathered to interrupt the job interviews. When the first senior tried to enter the room for an interview, he was turned away by a chain of interlocked arms. The same thing happened for two other students, who left amid a chorus of voices chanting "Workers, yes! GE, no!" Don McClain, the dean of students, was livid. He stood before the crowd and vowed to take the matter to the College Judicial Board for further action if the protesters didn't disband. When the students ignored him, McClain, frustrated, asked the recruiters to leave.

Within an hour, John Shay, the vice president for student affairs, read a statement on behalf of the college, noting that "the students who participated in [the] obstruction of the General Electric Company's career counseling appointment did so with the full knowledge that such obstruction was in direct defiance of an explicitly stated college policy on demonstrations." He added that anyone charged would have their cases heard before the College Judicial Board, which would have the authority to suspend or expel them. Later that day, members of McClain's staff made what they later called a "visual identification" of sixteen students out of the fifty-four who had been at the demonstration. They put the names of the identified protesters on a list of students to be charged with violating college rules. Most of the students on the list were activist

The protest against GE recruiters in front of Hogan Campus Center

organizers who had made a name for themselves at Holy Cross. Four of the sixteen identified students were black. They weren't regular protesters; they were merely, as McClain put it, "highly identifiable." There had been five black students in total at the demonstration.

Ted Wells organized an emergency BSU executive meeting that evening when he learned about the outcome of the demonstration. Wells thought the charges were racist, pure and simple. While most of the white students charged had organized the protest, the black students were just peripheral players. At the meeting Art Martin was visibly exasperated, and furious with the black protesters whose involvement was forcing the BSU to take a drastic stance. He described them as "badasses" and argued that it was their own fault if they were expelled, since the BSU had formally declined to participate in the protests. But he eventually agreed with Wells; the collective insult was too great to ignore. Clarence Thomas also felt torn. The school had set up a law, he argued, and these men had blatantly broken it. Still, he added, fair was fair, and in a crowd of mostly white men, the fact that it was easier to pick out the people with dark complexions didn't make it right. Thomas himself had contemplated going down to the demonstration. He shuddered to think that it could have been him—likely would have been him—about to face the judicial board if he had acted on his whim; this time he had ignored his usual instincts to oppose whatever stance Wells and the BSU put forward. In the end, all the men agreed that the college's behavior was unacceptable and racist. The board would have to drop all charges against the black men, or else the BSU would take action. None of them were willing to contemplate what kind of action they would take; they hoped that the college would understand the BSU's position and agree to its demands.

They decided to appoint a spokesman who would represent the black protesters before the judicial board. Each of the sixteen students would be making his individual case for why he shouldn't be suspended or expelled. It would be hard for any of them to argue that they didn't know they were breaking the rules, but the BSU wanted to make this a formal issue about race. Wells was passionate about how wronged the men were, and the BSU members agreed that nobody was better than Wells when it came to presenting a persuasive argument, not even Clarence Thomas. The accused students agreed to have Wells speak on their behalf.

The next morning, on December 11, Ted Wells left a message for Father Brooks, asking to meet before the 12:30 P.M. hearing. He believed the dean would share their outrage. Brooks didn't get the message in time, so Wells went to the meeting a half hour before it began and asked the board chairman, a larger-than-life chemistry professor named Michael McGrath, if he could represent the black students. A surprised McGrath turned to the four accused students to ask if they really thought that having another student explain their actions would help their case, and if they were sure they didn't want to speak up for themselves. The men nodded.

Wells immediately tried to shift the discussion away from the legality of the demonstrations. What they were there to talk about, he asserted, was "a much higher issue—racism." There had been fifty-four students at the demonstration, including five who were black. Of the sixteen who were singled out for punishment, though, a dozen were white and four were black. In other words, Wells noted, only 20 percent of the white demonstrators were charged, while 80 percent of the blacks were. "As spokesman for the Holy Cross BSU, I charge that this school has exhibited racist attitudes in the naming of a grossly disproportionate number of blacks to stand trial in this case," he told the room. Moreover, Wells noted that he was standing before a judicial board that was entirely white and, in all probability, unlikely to appreciate the inherent racism in how the students were charged.

The board, which consisted of one administrator, six professors, and three students, was silent after Wells's speech. Then they began to ask questions: Why were the black students at the protest? What were they doing during the demonstration? Were they members of the RSU? Weren't they standing near the door, where they would have been easy to identify—black or white? Did they want to have their cases looked at individually, so they could present extenuating circumstances, or did they want to be heard as a group? Each of the men responded that they wanted to be heard as a group. McGrath asked them again: Were they sure they wanted to stick with the group? They did. Several of the white students then jumped to their own defense, claiming that they had been charged only because of their involvement with the RSU and because they had been willing to give their names.

The board then began its deliberations. In an account later presented by McGrath, he noted that the members agreed that the rules had been broken, and debated whether the RSU itself had a right to exist, given its history of trampling on the rights of others. The fate of the black students was less clear. One member pointed out that just because they had been identified in higher numbers than the whites didn't mean they weren't subject to the same rules. But the fact that they had been singled out made some members uncomfortable, as did Ted Wells's warning that if amnesty weren't granted to the four men, the BSU would have "no alternative except to take action commensurate with the situation at hand."

Wells was worried when he walked out of the hearing. Back at the dorm he rounded up every member of the BSU to enlist their help in contacting all sixty-four black men on campus. Stan Grayson was away at a basketball game and couldn't be reached, and a few others were missing as well.

When the BSU met that night, the fury in the room was palpable. Wells wasn't optimistic about what the judicial board would decide. If its members didn't immediately see the racism of the situation, he believed, they probably never would.

The men began to yell out suggestions. "Let's blow something up," said one.

"Let's occupy a building."

"Let's march into Swords's office, man!"

Bob DeShay spoke calmly over the fray. "Let's just leave."

The men grew quiet. It was such a casual, yet compelling, suggestion. "Let's just leave," DeShay repeated. If the college didn't want them there, he argued, then why should they stay? There was no power in staging a sit-in, or marching to the president's office. But if they all got up and walked out together, that would really say something.

The men mulled over the suggestion. If they quit school, all of them might suffer. But the gesture would be impossible to ignore and, in one swift action, Holy Cross could lose its entire black student population. Clarence Thomas understood the risk in what his friend from Georgia was suggesting, and he was scared. He would have nowhere to go. There were scholarships on the line, and there would be heartbroken parents. But what choice did they have? If they weren't going to be treated fairly, he argued, the only answer was to calmly leave.

Art Martin sat quietly, staring at his hands. He was in his final year, headed to law school. He had endured three and a half years of studying, three and a half years of looking the other way at veiled insults. Graduation was in sight. But he couldn't let that stand in the way of doing what was right. "I'm in," he said.

Ted Wells had a lump in his throat as he thought about calling his mother, and about trying to get admitted to another good college on scholarship if he quit this one in protest.

Over the next few hours, they continued to debate strategy and give each student a chance to have his say. It was close to midnight when they finally put the matter to a vote. All of the men unanimously agreed to leave Holy Cross if the board declined the four protesters amnesty. It was the most powerful statement they could make, a test of the college's commitment to truly furthering civil rights. The college was important to the men, but they recognized that the black students were important to Holy Cross, too. Their presence, however small, was a visible testament to the dedication of Father Brooks and others to civil rights. They were taking a gamble: If the college wanted to make an example of four black men, it would lose them all.

Wells immediately called Brooks to explain their decision, and Brooks suggested that Wells and Martin meet him right away at the president's residence. When they arrived at 1:30 A.M., Brooks and President Swords were already waiting. The president listened as Wells and Martin explained the BSU's position, but although he acknowledged their concerns, he was unmoved by the argument. Nobody at the college should be allowed to disrupt legitimate campus activities and violate the rights of fellow students. Moreover, the decision lay in the hands of the members of the board. As president, he would abide by whatever they decided.

Brooks tried to find a middle ground, but he could see that there wasn't one. He argued to Wells and Martin that identifying the black students was likely less motivated by racism than by laziness, but he agreed that the results were the same. It was simply wrong to have such a high proportion of black students charged when most of the white students were exempt from punishment. But Swords wasn't about to dismiss charges against students who had broken the rules simply because they were black, either.

Brooks could see that the problem wasn't going to be resolved there. Even if the black students were willing to put their fates on the line over a matter of principle, the president wasn't about to give in. Brooks had witnessed how distraught his colleague and mentor had become amid what he saw as mounting chaos on campus and growing disrespect for the rules. Three months earlier, Swords had told Brooks that he couldn't go on any longer and was going to make preparations to leave at the end of the school year. The college was under financial strain, and the president had tapped its small endowment to raise faculty salaries. He had to deal with anger from alumni, faculty, and students who didn't like the form or the pace of change at Holy Cross. The stress had become too great.

Swords looked upset when he told the men that he couldn't make an exception for them.

"I guess that's it then," said Wells.

As he and Martin walked out the door, Brooks called after them, telling them not to do anything drastic. "Give us a chance to try to work things out."

Art Martin felt hurt and full of rage. The school wasn't even aware of its own racism, and Father Brooks, the man who had done so much to make them feel like a part of the community, now appeared to be utterly impotent.

Wells and Martin left their meeting with Swords at 2:45 A.M. on Friday, December 12. Fifteen minutes later, elsewhere on campus, the board announced its decision: All sixteen students charged would be suspended for the rest of the academic year; they had to pack up their bags and leave before 5 P.M. on Sunday. They would be allowed to take their exams for the final semester but they would not be allowed back on the campus for any other reason, though they would be allowed to apply for readmission to the college and resume their studies, with approval from the dean of men, in the fall of 1970. Wells and Martin walked over to the campus radio station and announced that, in response to the administration's decision, the black students were leaving Holy Cross. The BSU would hold a press conference at 10 A.M. to make its views known.

When they returned to the corridor, many of the men were still awake. They were devastated when they learned of the board's ruling. Wells suggested that they should all put on their best clothes in the morning, make their statement, and then walk proudly out of the school to start a new chapter of their lives. Several of the men began to call up the black freshmen who lived in the other dorms to inform them of the decision.

Eddie Jenkins felt passionate but also anxious about the walkout: He had already lost his football season and had barely recovered from hepatitis. It looked certain that he was off to Vietnam. Now he had to tell his parents that he would no longer be enrolled in the college that had made them so proud. His father had pushed hard for him to attend Holy Cross. Both parents would be crushed to learn that he quit.

Clarence Thomas sat in his room, anxiously deliberating over where he would go. Savannah was out of the question. He thought he might be able to spend a few nights in town at Kathy Ambush's house. He might find a way to continue his studies somewhere else, but it was the long term that worried him. What law school was going to accept and support a student who had dropped out because of alleged racism?

Ed Jones, though equally anxious, felt a surge of quiet pride in the BSU's willingness to stand together and fight racism. This was the kind of solidarity he had been calling for all year. As he later wrote in an article that ran in *National Catholic Reporter:* "Our concerns must begin to wander from the anxiety of getting a girl for the weekend to the future of black girls in the ghetto, from our grades to the total education of black people. If we fall into the ivory [white] tower bag, then we are doubly guilty of anything the whites are." If Jones hadn't come to Holy Cross, he firmly believed that he would have joined the Black Panthers in D.C. by now. But he was in Worcester, about to pack up his bags and leave his college education behind. He wasn't sure how his mother would react. While she was proud to have a son in college, she hadn't encouraged him to go. Jones knew that his life was a mystery to his mother. She wasn't the type to hope for too much. He imagined that if he quit and went home, she might just shrug, light up a cigarette, and tell him he better go find a job.

Ted Wells called his mother from a pay phone. Ma Wells was quiet while he explained what was going on. She trusted her son more than

Ted Wells announces the black students' decision to quit Holy Cross.

anyone in the world. "If you think it's the right thing to do, then that's what you should do," she said. Later Wells talked strategy with Art Martin: The men were to pack whatever belongings they could carry. In the morning they would walk together to the auditorium at the Hogan Campus Center and gather onstage to announce their departure. The BSU would pay for everyone's ticket home with cash on hand, which they would no longer need for anything else.

News of the planned walkout spread fast. The student government chairman held an emergency meeting and issued a statement condemning the "de facto racism" of the board's decision and calling for amnesty for all sixteen students. Several white students went to the corridor in support, as did a number of the black freshmen.

Father Brooks began fielding calls from parents before dawn. He understood their concern. Dropping out of college in the middle of the year would be damaging enough, but most of these men were also receiving full financial support from Holy Cross. Even if their sons were somehow able to return to the school, the parents were worried that the

Art Martin at the BSU press conference announcing the walkout

men's actions might jeopardize their scholarships. And in any case, they would be branded as reactionaries, which might jeopardize their future. Though he was scared for them, too, Brooks told them not to worry and promised that the college would do everything possible to work the crisis out.

By 10 A.M. Friday morning, more than six hundred students had gathered in the Hogan ballroom. There was a sense of anticipation in the air, the feeling that something dramatic was going to happen. Most of the students had come out to support the BSU's stance. Fearful about Vietnam and disillusioned with the establishment, many of the students felt a bond with the men who had the courage to stand up to authority. The crowd erupted in cheers as the black students filed in and walked up onto the stage. With the exception of three or four students, every black man on campus had agreed to join in the walkout. Brooks stood to the side looking grim as Wells read a statement.

The BSU sympathized with the Revolutionary Students Union in its struggle against human oppression, he said, but this was about racism. It was about the arbitrary decision to charge 80 percent of the black students at a demonstration and let 80 percent of the white students go free. The black students of Holy Cross had no choice but to walk away from the college until the four men in question were reinstated without punishment.

When Wells finished speaking, the men behind him raised their arms with clenched fists in a sign of black power. Then, one by one, they threw down their student ID cards and walked single file out of the ballroom. As they left, the other students in the room began to chant "Strike!" and other words of support. Brooks pushed his way through the ballroom to reach Wells outside, and asked him to please keep everyone close by. He was going to find a way to work everything out. Wells told Brooks that they had made their position clear. Brooks nodded. He would do what he could, but Wells and Martin, at least, had to be willing to stay close by to negotiate. Wells agreed.

Much of the student body was now threatening to boycott classes unless the black students returned. More important, Brooks felt that

Photo of the walkout published in *The Crusader* on December 19, 1969

they couldn't let every one of those men walk away from their education. "There are times," he told the president, "when one principle has to override another." To Brooks's surprise, Swords agreed. Brooks learned that a few members of the College Judicial Board were even reconsidering their decision. Brooks offered to help gather a group together to discuss the situation with Swords so that the president could reconsider the facts of the case. He knew they needed to act quickly.

His top priority was to find a person to join the discussions who could represent the views of the black students. He approached John Scott, a respected black community activist and former sociology professor who was also chairman of the city of Worcester's Human Rights Committee. Paul Rosenkrantz and Brooks would be part of the group, along with John Shay, who had been on the judicial board but had abstained from voting. Others would be invited to join in and speak, when appropriate. On the surface the goal was to present all points of view, but for Brooks it was to bring the black students back before it was too late.

As Brooks rushed to assemble the group, the black students dispersed in different directions. About half the students went to Clark University to camp out on dorm room floors. The rest left Worcester, and many of the students went to Clark or tried to stay locally to see if they'd be heading home on Sunday night.

At 4:00 P.M., Swords and Brooks went to a scheduled meeting of the Board of Trustees, which informed Swords that it wasn't their role to reverse the decision of any campus group. Swords was the only one with the authority to do that.

Brooks went to see Ted Wells and Art Martin to explain what was going on. They knew John Scott and felt that, as someone who was black and not affiliated with Holy Cross, he would be sympathetic to their arguments. They agreed to negotiate through him. As Brooks turned to leave, he thrust a couple of hundred dollars into Wells's hand. When Wells looked up in surprise, Brooks asked him to spread it among the men. They wouldn't be eating on campus for a while, Brooks pointed out, so they could use the money to get some burgers and fries. Wells suspected that the money had come from the priest's own pocket.

As Brooks anxiously tried to resolve the situation, he was reminded of the time he had spent in Rome during the early days of Vatican II. When a prominent biblical scholar, Father Stanislas Lyonnet, S.J., had been pulled out of Brooks's class for being too radical, he and several classmates had printed up bulletins and distributed them around the Vatican to defend his stance. After much lobbying, Brooks and his colleagues had managed to get Lyonnet reinstated. Brooks understood the power of standing together to uphold a principle. He believed that some good could come of the BSU's protest, but his immediate goal was to make sure that the students' academic careers weren't destroyed. What mattered now was that Swords was willing to hear the other side's arguments.

Protester in the strike that followed the walkout

Stan Grayson didn't learn about the walkout until later that evening, when the basketball players returned from an embarrassing 92–68 loss to Columbia. Grayson was exhausted and bracing himself for some ribbing about the team's defeat. As he got off the bus, he saw Ted Wells, who explained what had happened. Grayson immediately told his teammates that he had to leave.

The team was scheduled to play more games in the coming days, but Coach Donohue told him to do whatever he thought was right. Grayson was one of the coach's favorite players; the coach admired the sophomore's principles and integrity. Grayson shook his coach's hand, and the hands of his team members, and immediately headed to the corridor to grab his things.

Grayson didn't want to sleep on a floor at Clark University, so he and Eddie Jenkins borrowed a friend's car and drove to Boston. When they arrived at a nightclub called Estelle's, they were in an oddly jubilant mood. It struck Grayson that he might never be coming back to Holy Cross, and that thought made him feel free. He didn't want to contemplate what might come next; he just felt relief to be away from the stress of the crisis in Worcester. He and Jenkins drank and danced, mingling with the locals. The next morning, weary and hungover, they drove back to Worcester to see if anything had been resolved.

The campus was buzzing with activity. A number of students and faculty had organized a daylong forum to talk about the racism charges. Father Brooks had brought together the advisory committee that morning. President Swords sat silently as John Scott, the arbitrator, got up and warned that "if you let these men quit, then it's likely that a lot of other students will walk out and you'll have a general strike on your hands." That might draw the SDS, Black Panthers, or other activist groups intent on stirring up violence. Swords listened but remained silent. Brooks understood that the president wanted to witness the debate, not influence it. For the rest of Saturday and into the night, Swords didn't offer a single opinion.

Clarence Thomas had packed his bags in anticipation of leaving campus forever, but he was relieved to hear that Father Brooks had intervened in the negotiations. While the other men were still talking in apocalyptic terms about their futures, Thomas had a feeling that Holy Cross wasn't going to let almost all of its black students—the ones they had fought so hard to recruit and accommodate—just walk out the door on principle. There was no way Father Brooks would let that happen. President Swords may have felt a need to stick to the rules, but Thomas trusted Brooks. There was no denying that the suspension had been a racist act; surely Swords would see that the black students had no choice. Thomas was hoping he wouldn't need to confront his grandfather with another failure.

At the forum, emotions were still running high. Some faculty members were visibly angry that the black students were getting special treatment; another admitted that he had initially opposed amnesty but then reversed his decision when he saw the severity of the sentence. Now he

A student protest in response to the walkout

didn't see why any of the black students would want to return to Holy Cross after the treatment that they had received.

The *Worcester Telegram* ran an editorial on Saturday praising the board for its "courage" in sticking to its guns and noting that the rules had been "arrogantly flouted by a group of self-styled revolutionary students who almost precipitated mob violence in a crowded corridor." Black or white, the *Telegram* wrote, the students deserved to be punished.

During every break from the council discussions, Father Brooks drove to the Clark campus to tell Ted Wells and Art Martin what had happened in the meetings. He wanted to make sure that the men didn't lose hope and start to disperse. He asked Wells if the men needed anything. His voice cracking with fatigue, Brooks promised to call with updates. Wells agreed to persuade everyone to stay put; he knew the stakes were too high to do otherwise.

Although he was moved by the priest's commitment, Wells was still angry. Brooks might care about the fate of the BSU, but the fact that the president hadn't reversed his decision yet was upsetting. What was clear-cut racism to the black students seemed to be a gray area to the leaders of Holy Cross. Why else would they still be debating the matter?

Wells was right—many in the Holy Cross administration saw no need to welcome the black students back. The discussions among members of the advisory group were getting heated. Some faculty members felt that overruling the College Judicial Board would be tantamount to calling it worthless and letting the campus degenerate into mob rule. It would be a victory for the demonstrators. But Brooks didn't much care about whether the president's ruling might prompt further demonstrations or damage to the school's reputation; the real tragedy of getting it wrong would be felt by the students.

The group took a break at 2:30 A.M., and Brooks drove back to Clark to meet again with Wells and Martin. They told him that many of the black students would head home Sunday night if the president hadn't reversed his decision by that point, and they would do the same, too. When Brooks let the committee know of the black students' intentions, several remained unmoved. As he later told Worcester's *Evening Gazette*, sometimes whites "couldn't even see their own bias, never mind overcome it."

As the sun was beginning to set on Sunday afternoon, President Swords announced that he had heard enough. Brooks contacted Wells and Martin to ask that they return to the school to hear the president's decision.

At 6:30 P.M. on December 14, Swords and Brooks arrived at the ballroom, where hundreds of students and faculty had already gathered. Swords looked somber as he stepped up to the podium. Everyone was silent as the president stood up, adjusted the thick, black frames of his glasses, and read his statement. "I am granting amnesty to the sixteen students of Holy Cross College whose suspension from the College because of their involvement in the General Electric Company incident was previously announced." Every student who had been charged in the demonstration, black or white, would be exonerated and free to resume their studies.

The murmurs of the crowd almost drowned out the rest of his words. Swords went on to say that he now agreed with the BSU that the procedures for identifying students weren't ideal and that every student who had been at the protest should have been charged. While the judicial board may have acted as fairly as it could have under the circumstances, its decision would be reversed. Moreover, all campus recruitment would be postponed and formal classes would be canceled for the following week to allow students and faculty to discuss racial issues on campus. Everyone had been affected by the events of the past three days, and Swords wanted to give the campus time to absorb them and a chance to debate their opinions.

Brooks felt a wave of relief, and respect for Swords's courage to reverse his public stance. Art Martin and Ted Wells, standing near the stage, dressed in jackets and ties, were visibly moved. As the crowd cheered, Martin came to the podium to announce that the black students would return to campus after the Christmas break. One of the students saw Brooks standing to the side, slipping out quietly with tears in his eyes.

TEN

What Do You Fight For?

Predictably, anger erupted over President Raymond Swords's decision. There were pointed editorials in the *Worcester Telegram* that claimed the amnesty had "severely damaged the credibility of the college administration" and letters printed in *The Crusader* alleging that Holy Cross had been raped by the president and that "the avowed rapist is one of her own sons." A businessman propped a casket outside the main gate of the college with a sign that read, "Here lies the corpse of free enterprise, born July 4, 1776, laid to rest by Raymond J. Swords, S.J., Dec. 15, 1969." Father Brooks stepped up to support the president and handle the criticism. When the letters from irate alumni and parents poured in, demanding answers and accusing Swords of being spineless, Brooks dealt with the critics. The president didn't have the energy to deal with any more conflict himself.

As 1969 came to a close and a new decade dawned, the stress of the walkout intensified Swords's desire to step down as president. Swords wanted Brooks to consider taking over his job and Brooks felt honored. In his view Swords had been magnificent as president, daring to alienate fellow Jesuits by removing them from faculty jobs for more qualified outsiders. He had been willing to test his own boundaries and had exercised his power wisely. The decision to grant amnesty to the GE protesters had gone against Swords's personal beliefs regarding discipline and respect, but he had done it because it was the right thing to do.

But while the experience of appeasing angry alumni and weighing moral issues against practical ones may have drained Swords, Brooks had never had a problem defending himself against people he believed were wrong. Arguments that had been percolating during the black student recruitment drive now came out into the open: For many, the amnesty became emblematic of all that was wrong with efforts to accommodate black students. One alumnus accused Brooks of letting the "colored boys" dictate how the college should be run, and argued that he was rewarding the students' disrespect for the rules. The alumnus claimed that Brooks and Swords had given Holy Cross a reputation for being a place that gave Negroes special treatment, and had put all of its students at a disadvantage by letting recruiters know that the school would tolerate demonstrations.

Brooks spent weeks traveling around the country to meet with different alumni groups. The angry letters were handed to him to answer, as were the irate phone calls. When newspaper reporters called, they found themselves interviewing Father Brooks. He met with the professors who felt betrayed by the school's reversal, and with the students who were quietly troubled by the decision. Parents weren't sure if they should let their sons apply for the following year and called Brooks to demand an explanation. In each case he tried to assure them that the college had not abandoned its standards, stressing that the injustice didn't lie in the charges against the protesters but in how those charges had been handed out. Were such demonstrations ever to happen again, he assured them, the administration would take extra care to make sure that every perpetrator was punished, black and white. But Brooks refused to tolerate any suggestion that the black students had been wrong to walk out or that Holy Cross had been wrong to accept them back. One student at the time later recalled a conversation with a professor who had complained to Brooks about the perils of rewarding what he saw as the BSU's tantrum, only to have Brooks respond that he'd love to see that caliber of childish behavior among the faculty. While comforting or cajoling alumni may have been tolerable to Brooks, expending similar energy on his colleagues was out of the question. "You always got the sense he'd forge ahead, whether you liked it or not," a professor from that period noted. "I remember mentioning a mutual colleague who'd had real qualms about how the walkout was handled, and Father Brooks saying, 'that's his problem.'"

The black students returned to Holy Cross with mixed feelings. Some worked harder; others found it difficult to get back into the school routine. Al Coleman, one of the black protesters who had dodged a suspension, had promised Brooks that he would stop cutting classes after his reinstatement. He didn't. Coleman ended up dropping out of school, though with nowhere to go he continued to live on the black corridor until the end of the year, reading his science fiction books, eating food that the other men brought over from Kimball, and continuing to attend the Sunday BSU meetings. Jenkins suspected that Brooks and others in the administration knew that Coleman was still living on campus but nobody bothered to officially kick him out. Brooks had become a more regular presence on the corridor, stopping by to check in on the men, who greeted him with enthusiasm. Clarence Thomas, in particular, seemed to light up when he saw Father Brooks around the residence. They often sat together and talked about what was going on in the world. Ted Wells's status had increased on campus because of his prominent role in the walkout; his name had appeared with some frequency in the press, and he continued to speak on behalf of the BSU. During the weeklong forum that Holy Cross held for students and faculty following the walkout, Wells was a commanding presence. "Black students cannot afford the luxury of learning just for the sake of learning," he told a crowd, according to a report in the *Worcester Telegram*. They were in college to get the skills to "destroy this sick society and replace it with one that will be functional to the needs of black people," he added. "The college must realize that black students do not want to be indoctrinated into well-rounded white men, but that we wish to be educated in the art of achieving manhood." The BSU's dramatic stance against racism had reinforced in Wells the conviction that he was at Holy Cross not just to get ahead in his career, but to change society. He embraced his leadership role, and other students came to view him as a spokesman on the black student experience.

The question was whether he had embraced the role too much. While Wells had stepped up his commitment because Art Martin had felt a need to cut back, the younger man hadn't officially asked the men in the BSU for a bigger role. It was simply a logical transition, given Wells's position as a deputy the year before, as well as the clear leadership he had displayed during the crisis. But the automatic rise of Wells didn't go unnoticed by other BSU members. While nobody else had stepped forward to seek the job when the matter came up at a meeting in early 1970, many thought it felt wrong to approach the transfer of power like a coronation instead of putting it to a vote. To some, what had come across as inspiring leadership during the walkout now seemed to teeter on smugness. While Wells didn't sense that anything had changed, other BSU members thought it might be time to knock the ambitious sophomore down a few pegs.

Still, when the matter of who would run the union came to a vote, Wells's was the only name under consideration. In a surprise move, Clarence Thomas suddenly came forward to challenge him. Thomas didn't particularly want to take a leadership role—he much preferred to stay on the sidelines, tossing barbs to stir things up—but some men in the Georgia contingent had talked him into it. After the men cast their votes, Eddie Jenkins counted the ballots and for a moment looked surprised. When he announced that Thomas had won, the room was quiet. Eddie Jenkins glanced over at Wells, who looked visibly shaken, though he was clearly trying to take the defeat in stride. If the goal had been to humble Wells, Jenkins thought, they had succeeded.

A mixture of clapping and murmuring broke out, and then one of the men from Georgia approached Jenkins in private to say that Thomas really did not want the job. He would happily concede the election should some technicality force a new vote. "I wasn't interested in running anything," Thomas later recalled. "We just felt someone should give Ted a run for his money, and that ended up being me."

They decided that the first vote had in fact been for the nomination. The men would have to cast a second vote for the actual election. There was a motion to cast new ballots. On the second round of voting, Wells won. This time Thomas looked visibly relieved, though some men said they also detected a twinge of irritation on his face. Thomas, though, insisted he felt nothing but relief, saying he didn't want to hold any of-

Wells appointed new BSU chairman

Ted Wells, a sophomore economics major, has been elected chairman of the Black Students Union for the 1970 academic year, "succeeding Art Martin, who chaired the Union in its first year.

Wells stated that the BSU would continue its cooperative program with the BSU of Clark University working with the black youth in Worcester at the Prospect House Center. "We plan to increase our work at the Prospect House and aim at greater black awareness among the brothers there."

"As for the plans of the BSU on campus, we have told the admissions department that ten per cent of the class of 1974 should be black." Wells added that the BSU would continue to try to make

Ted Wells

"life liveable" for the blacks on campus this year.

Article in *The Crusader* about Ted Wells being appointed BSU chairman

ficial role in the BSU. He had other things on his plate. Kathy Ambush had been feeling unhappy and isolated at Anna Maria, and she and Thomas increasingly opted to spend weekends hanging out at her parents' house in Worcester. Even after the walkout, Thomas still felt that Holy Cross was a place more to be endured than enjoyed. The comforts of the corridor hadn't disguised the fact that he found the views of many of his hallmates to be increasingly dogmatic and one-dimensional; his camaraderie with the white students on campus didn't diminish the discomfort he felt at not belonging.

If anything, though, the loneliness sharpened his focus. He continued to excel in intramural football and track, though the sight of Eddie Jenkins, Joe Wilson, and Jaffe Dickerson racing by him on the track in jest one day was a reminder that athletics wasn't his life. Thomas had been invited to join the prestigious Purple Key Society, a group comprised of top-performing students that tried to raise school spirit and help others on campus. He had also been appointed to Alpha Sigma Nu, the national Jesuit college honor society, at Father Brooks's request. Brooks had written a letter to Raymond Swords, recommending that the president appoint Thomas, as "Clarence has a cumulative quality point index of 3.577 and ranks very high in his class," adding that Thomas was "genuinely respected by his fellow students." Brooks believed strongly that the hardworking junior deserved the recognition, but that wasn't his only motivation. Having spent time talking to Thomas about his frustrations and insecurities, Brooks also sensed that he needed it.

While Thomas's interest in writing articles for *The Crusader* took a backseat to other commitments, Ed Jones discovered that writing was his passion. Jones's newspaper column gave him an outlet for his anger, but it was a course in the nineteenth-century novel that nurtured his love of storytelling. His English professor, Maurice Geracht, was immediately struck by the speed with which Jones read the assigned books, as well as by the beauty of the sophomore's prose. Geracht later invited Jones to be a part of the college's first-ever creative writing class. Jones,

Clarence Thomas with other members of the Purple Key Society

meanwhile, was inspired by the way that Geracht approached the craft of writing and was flattered by his praise. While other professors were lukewarm about Jones's work, Geracht told Jones that he had a gift. After reading *Dubliners*, a collection of short stories by the Irish author James Joyce, Jones felt he had discovered a calling: He wanted to do for Washington, D.C., what Joyce had done for Dublin, to bring the city to life and give voice to its people.

Ted Wells, meanwhile, had his hands full as chairman of the BSU. It wasn't long before the black freshmen who had been living in the regular first-year residences were complaining to him that they felt lonely. Wells asked Father Brooks to let some of the freshmen move in with black roommates or move to the black corridor, but Brooks opposed the idea on the grounds that the room changes might cause chaos in the other residences, and leave some wounded egos among the roommates who were left behind. Brooks was irritated that the freshmen weren't even willing to give the broader college experience a try, but he also recognized that some of the men who were now sophomores had found the

isolation of their freshman year to be particularly trying, so much so
that it affected their success in school. Once again Brooks let the BSU
have its way. Wells sent the offer out to all freshman members of the
BSU to let them know that the school was willing to let them move, but
in the end only a small number of the black freshmen were willing to
disrupt their routines or abandon their white roommates to achieve a
measure of comfort.

Brooks also told Wells that he would allow the BSU to reach out to
incoming freshmen the following year, allowing them a chance to opt in
advance for a black roommate. It was a mirror image of the dubious
outreach that had so enraged the men a year earlier, when administrators had asked white students if they would mind living with a black
man. Now the BSU was insisting that black students be given the option
to reject a roommate based on skin color. Wells again convinced the
dean that creating a comfort zone for new black students would ease the
transition. Still, Brooks hoped the segregated living experiment would
fail. He rejected the idea of a "Black Judicial Board" that could rule on
matters involving black students and over which the BSU leadership—in
this case, Ted Wells—would have veto power. But on many of the key
issues, Brooks agreed. Wells had personally approached the admissions
office to ask that the school admit fifty-seven black students in the class
of 1974—about 10 percent of the total number of admitted students. In
a note to the admissions director, Brooks argued that the BSU's request
sounded reasonable, as the college had identified 108 black students
who had expressed interest in attending Holy Cross, of whom sixty appeared to meet the school's admissions standards and twenty-five would
likely be acceptable under the standards they'd adopted for admitting
blacks to the class of 1973. That allowed for the consideration of special
factors that might dampen formal test results, such as family hardship
or the quality of the high school education that a student had received.
The concern for Brooks was whether the students could receive adequate
preparation to bring their academics up to speed. Special consideration
in granting admission was not the same thing as special consideration in

granting grades. Allowing the latter, Brooks firmly believed, would be toxic to everyone, especially the students themselves.

The challenge, as always, was finding the money. Campus visits for potential recruits had become too expensive. The school was in a tough spot. To satisfy all the requests for financial aid the following year, it would need around $450,000, and there was less than $150,000 available. As it was, Holy Cross was going into the next school year with a planned deficit of $1.4 million, and that figure already factored in a $350 increase in tuition. Over the previous two years, the budget for scholarships and grants had increased by a third, to more than $1 million, in part due to the significant increase in aid for black students.

While Brooks didn't share his financial concerns with Wells, he did convey some of his frustrations. Wells was succeeding at Holy Cross, as were most of the others. But some of the black students were continuing to struggle, and were on the cusp of dropping out. The issue, in most cases, wasn't intelligence or grades. Some of the black students who weren't happy, Brooks concluded, hadn't been adequately prepared for the realities of college life.

Efforts to stop the Vietnam War had taken on even greater urgency after the lottery. Clarence Thomas joined several of the men that spring to take part in an antiwar rally in Cambridge. They parked the van near the Harvard University campus and joined a crowd that was marching toward Harvard Square, shouting "Ho! Ho! Ho Chi Minh" to protest the treatment of America's domestic political prisoners. On the way, they passed a liquor store where the owner was giving away free drinks. As Thomas recalled in his memoir, he wasn't sure if the man supported the antiwar cause or if he was simply trying to build goodwill to avoid having his windows smashed. Whatever his motivation, the men stopped long enough for Thomas and some of the others to get drunk. With a little more wobble in their stride, they continued marching until they came upon a group of policemen wearing riot gear and wielding billy clubs. The officers fired tear gas into the crowd and then walked up to where Thomas and the other men from the corridor were standing. "This must be the nigger contingent from Roxbury," Thomas recalled one of them saying. The students turned around, walked briskly to the car, and drove back to Worcester as fast as they could. Thomas vowed to never take part in a public demonstration again. He had had enough of the angry mob.

Meanwhile, Thomas was struggling to figure out where he stood on issues of social justice. While he still saw himself as an essentially left-wing thinker devoted to addressing social wrongs—when books by black conservatives came his way, he immediately threw them in the trash—he had grown tired of the standard-issue radical rhetoric. As he later said, "I just fundamentally disagreed with the in-your-face approach to everything." He didn't buy into the conspiracy theories about the war, and he disliked the constant rage that the other BSU members expressed. He was especially critical of the assumption that every brother had to think and act the same way. He found it all too simplistic and immature.

As he looked around for a better philosophy, Thomas found himself intrigued by the half dozen Black Muslims who were living on campus. They were sharp dressers, almost always seen in the crisp white shirts and bow ties advocated by the Nation of Islam movement. They also ate well, eventually getting Brooks's help in setting up their own menus and permission to prepare food in the corridor. Thomas liked that the men weren't in any way frivolous. When they weren't studying, they were usually praying or traveling to the Boston mosque where the Roxbury-raised Louis Farrakhan had gained fame as a minister a few years earlier. Some of the other men on the corridor would enjoy a laugh at their expense, shouting sarcastic responses like, "Yes sir, brother," or "You say it, brother" when their earnestness became too much to take, but Thomas admired the Muslim students' mantra of self-reliance, the philosophy that the black man had to shift his focus from buying things to building them; from hurting one another to helping one another. Only then could he hope to control his destiny, gain self-respect, and avoid going back to the white man for handouts. Every time the Muslim students went to Boston, they would bring back bean pies and issues of the popular *Muhammad Speaks* newspaper to sell to other men on the corridor. To Thomas, it demonstrated an admirable work ethic, but he couldn't ascribe to their philosophy of militant separatism. It seemed futile and naïve.

Eddie Jenkins was finding himself increasingly paralyzed with anxiety over Vietnam. He was worried about being called up and, as he feared, his draft notice arrived soon after he returned to school in January. He was lifting weights when someone brought him the envelope, and he knew what it was without even opening it. His father, the mailman in their neighborhood, had taught him how to detect a draft notice. After working-class recipients had complained that they couldn't afford transportation to the draft board, the city had started including subway tokens with draft letters. All his father had to do was feel the weight of the letter to know that he was bearing an unwelcome delivery. Jenkins instantly felt the token in his own package.

Jenkins slipped into a funk. He had known for weeks that his low number meant a trip to Vietnam, but he hadn't expected the call to service to arrive so soon. He was due to appear before the draft board at Fort Hamilton in New York City just a few weeks later, where the board would determine if he was fit to fight. President Richard Nixon had promised in his 1968 campaign that he would end the draft, but nobody thought he would deliver on his promise anytime soon—and, regardless, it certainly wouldn't happen soon enough to make a difference to Jenkins.

The men on the corridor tried to cheer up Eddie with jokes and gave him advice on how to handle the interview. Jenkins tried to make light of his situation—he'd get the chance to escape another winter in Worcester and meet the beautiful women of Asia—but he was so scared that he started having nightmares. Jenkins wasn't about to lie his way out of it, as some other recruits tried to do. He wouldn't claim to be a conscientious objector based on his religious beliefs—American Catholics had clearly shown a tolerance for war. He didn't have a criminal record, and nobody on the draft board would believe him if he claimed to be homosexual, an exclusion that was proving hard to get even for men who were. He wasn't a teacher, a farmer, or in the National Guard, and he hadn't fathered any children that he knew of. Jenkins couldn't think of any scenario in which a healthy football player could avoid serving in Vietnam.

When Jenkins arrived at the recruitment office in New York, some protesters outside the building told him to try to get every answer wrong, so that he would be disqualified on intellectual grounds. Inside the waiting area, a man played a haunting soundtrack on the harmonica. Once in the office, a middle-aged man handed Jenkins a qualifying test to fill out. Watching him, the man raised his eyebrows. "Son, I know what you're trying to do here," he said. "But I should tell you that we've been through all this since Muhammad Ali."

Ali had lost his career when he refused to serve in Vietnam. If that's how they treated a celebrity, Jenkins wondered what they would do to a no-name black kid like him. As harmonica music droned on in the background, the man informed Jenkins that he could be a certified idiot and the army would gladly let him in. "But here's what getting all the answers wrong will do," the man continued. "It will mess up your chances of becoming an officer." Jenkins, who never thought that playing dumb would be a viable strategy, sat down to do the best job he could.

At his physical exam, a physician asked him to do a knee bend. Jenkins did one, but he winced slightly. The doctor told him to do it again. "We have a problem," the man said. "Do you have something wrong with your knees?" Jenkins explained that his knee had been operated on and he had done some rehab. It didn't usually bother him much, but he wasn't about to say so. The doctor stared at his leg as if summoning up a mental picture of Jenkins crawling through the jungle on his problem knee. Jenkins detected a look of sympathy in the man's eyes. He said a silent prayer as the doctor asked him to do a knee bend again. "I don't think so," the doctor said when Jenkins came up to his full height. "I think you may be a candidate for a 1-Y status."

When Jenkins returned to Holy Cross, the parties, the jostling in the hall, even the fights took on a sweeter tone. A week later a letter arrived to inform him that the injury had rendered him unable to serve. He wasn't going to go to Vietnam. The raucous and wisecracking Eddie J. was back.

Eddie Jenkins's personal good fortune didn't take away from the reality that the political mood on campus was increasingly somber. Holy Cross, perhaps owing to both its prestige and its convenient location, had become a popular stop for political activists on campus tours, but opinions about the school from its guest speakers weren't always favorable. The "Yippie" leader Abbie Hoffman returned to his hometown to speak at the Field House and called Holy Cross a "minimum-security penitentiary." The only good thing the activist could bring himself to say about the college was that counterculture guru Timothy Leary had studied there. Jenkins was intrigued by the Black Panther who'd come and scoffed at their reports of the walkout. "You brothers are wasting your time," he told them. "The only thing the Man understands is a gun." As proof, he pulled one out of his pocket. He suggested the BSU blow the buildings up and threaten violence. Jenkins could barely stifle his laughter. Jenkins remained passionate in his politics but he was increasingly aware that some of the people around him were more invested in the cause than he was. That became even clearer to him after arguing with a white basketball player about social injustice. The student insisted that he and Jenkins were brothers because Irish suffering was just like black suffering. "Catholics are the niggers of Northern Ireland," the man told Jenkins. "We're connected." Jenkins responded that he didn't know there had been slaves in Ireland. He debated mentioning that his white grandfather had come from Ireland, but he decided that he couldn't be bothered.

Jenkins agreed to witness what the group of Irish American kids was doing to help their comrades across the Atlantic in what became known as "The Troubles," a period of violent clashes between Catholic and

Protestant militants in Northern Ireland. The basketball player picked Jenkins up in a battered old car a few days later and handed him a wool cap to pull over his eyes as he jumped into the backseat.

"What's this for?" Jenkins asked.

"Put it on!" another man barked. "It's for your own protection."

There were two other white men in the car, and Jenkins suddenly felt nervous, wondering if the rhetoric about Irish liberation was a ruse, a front for a group devoted to bringing down the system. Then again, he thought, who would kidnap someone in Worcester? He pulled the cap down to his nose and sat back in the seat, trying to look as if he was enjoying himself.

About eight minutes later they stopped on a suburban street. Jenkins thought maybe they had driven around the block several times to make the distance seem farther. The men led him out of the car and down into a basement, where Jenkins took off the wool cap. Lying before him were dozens of guns and rounds of ammunition. In another corner of the room there were white sheets draped across what looked to be more caches of weapons, as well as a table laden with tinned hams.

"What's all this for?" Jenkins asked.

"It's for the fight, brother," said one young man with a thick Belfast accent. "We're raising money and sending supplies to the Irish Republican Army. We're fighting for our homeland."

Jenkins's Holy Cross companion immediately launched into a speech about how the British government was destroying the Catholic people, the same British government that had forced Jenkins's people into slavery, and how the Irish Catholics had been oppressed for generations, just like the blacks. "Martin Luther King is our hero, too," said the man. "We're brothers in the fight against oppression."

It seemed that everyone on campus had a cause to support, and the political atmosphere was about to get even more tense. On April 30, 1970, Richard Nixon announced that U.S. troops were invading Cambodia to cut off supply routes to the North Vietnamese. America was deeply divided about the war, but especially its younger people. While those under thirty were the loudest opponents of the war, in polls conducted between 1965 and 1971 they reported the highest percentage of support for it. A common complaint was that the United States hadn't done enough to try to win the war. While 55 percent of Americans said the war had been a mistake, by 1969 a substantial minority still felt it was their duty to support the military and its efforts in Vietnam. Despite promises from Washington to train more Vietnamese allies to defend the South, allowing U.S. troops to pull out, the war seemed to be shifting in the North's favor. Less than a week after Nixon's announcement, on May 4, the Student-Faculty Senate at Holy Cross voted to hold a weeklong strike of classes to protest against the deployment of troops to Cambodia. Father Brooks spoke out vehemently against the war, but he reminded students that they should find peaceful ways to express their views. The same day, four students at Kent State University in Ohio were shot and killed by National Guardsmen who were sent to quell a demonstration. Riots and protests broke out on campuses across the country.

Suddenly, to most of the students, nothing felt more important than stopping the war. Holy Cross canceled classes for the week. On May 5, about two hundred angry students gathered outside the Air Force ROTC building in protest. Brooks guarded the door as President Swords spoke to the students and eventually convinced them to disperse without damaging the building. Ted Wells, Eddie Jenkins, and several other men on the corridor drove the BSU van to Washington to march on the White House. Ma Wells took them all in for the night.

A few days later six black men were killed during a race riot in Augusta, Georgia. Five of them were shot by police. On May 14, police opened fire on Jackson State University students protesting racism on the Mississippi campus, killing two black men and wounding a dozen others. One of the victims was a pre-med student who left behind a baby son and a pregnant wife; the other was just a teenager who had stopped to watch the riots.

In the spring of 1970, Swords gave what would be his last address to the senior class. He talked about the "catalytic events of the past six weeks" and argued that, "from this point on, there is no turning back, no copping out. You have made your stand, openly and publicly, for all to see. It is a stand for life, for peace, for justice for all men." Like most colleges across the nation, Holy Cross had coped with escalating political tensions but had been spared any kind of violence. The recent events were largely abstract: There had been no riot police, no National Guard, and nobody had been arrested, beaten, or killed.

At the end of the school year, the Board of Trustees announced that Father John Brooks, now forty-six, had been chosen to be the twenty-fifth president of Holy Cross College. After a nine-month search involving sixty applicants, the trustees had finally settled on the man Raymond Swords had always wanted to replace him. They noted Brooks's master of arts degree in philosophy and master of science in geophysics, as well as his doctorate of sacred theology from the Gregorian Pontifical University of Rome. The new president was also an active member of the Worcester NAACP branch.

While Swords had worked tirelessly to improve the school, it was time for new leadership. The trustees argued that John Brooks was a man who could maintain the intellectual and religious traditions of the college while also leading it in a new direction. As a new decade was beginning, Holy Cross needed a leader who was unafraid to move with the times, and it needed a president who could not only embrace change but accelerate it.

As he had promised Ted Wells earlier in the year, Brooks allowed the BSU to send letters to the incoming black freshmen in the class of 1974. Malcolm Joseph, the BSU vice chairman, wrote up the letters, informing the recruits that the BSU had "convinced the Administration, that it would be best for your interests if you were given the option of expressing your preference of a black or white roommate before the school year started. This will undoubtedly save you needless aggravation."

Art Martin felt wistful as his graduation approached. Four years earlier he had arrived, feeling isolated, until Brooks had reached out to ask for his help in spreading the message of Holy Cross to other black students. The arrival of that first group of recruits had transformed Martin's life on campus from one of loneliness to one of brotherhood. The founding BSU chairman felt he owed much of that transformation to Father Brooks, who had been there for Martin before and after there was a black community on campus. Brooks hadn't reached out to Martin because of what he did or who he represented; he had kept his door open, Martin reflected later, because he knew that a young black student from Newark might need to know that there was someone he could turn to. Martin was on his way to Georgetown University's law school, where he would go on to chair the Black American Law Students Association and eventually become both a lawyer specializing in job discrimination and deputy attorney general for New Jersey. In 1970, as he went by Father Brooks's office to shake the new president's hand and say goodbye, Martin felt he was leaving a friend.

That summer, Brooks had many long conversations with Clarence Thomas and Gil Hardy, whom he'd helped move into a college-owned house over the break. Hardy was dating a local young woman, Vivianne Townes, and Thomas was deeply in love with Ambush. The four of them spent most evenings talking for hours into the night. When there was a fifth member of the group, Townes recalls, it was often Father Brooks, who would drop by for a drink and then stay on to talk about what was happening in the world.

The priest had come to believe strongly that simply being aware of racism was inadequate. He had been aware of racism all his life, and yet, he realized, for too long he hadn't done enough to address it. Talk was meaningless if nothing changed. What mattered to Brooks was personal responsibility. Once a person was aware of a problem, it was his or her moral and spiritual responsibility to help solve it. The tragedies of the Holocaust or lynchings or oppression lay not just in the acts, Brooks argued, but in the inaction of the people who stood by. Awareness might help the world, but it would never change it.

Brooks had come to feel a personal responsibility for the black students at Holy Cross. It wasn't a responsibility for their success; the choice to study and do the work was theirs alone, as it was for every student. It was a responsibility to acknowledge that the college experience might not be as comfortable for the black students, that they didn't have the role models in the classroom or the easy comfort of being in the majority. It also wasn't an impulse to set lower or higher expectations for the students, but to do something that seemed even more difficult for some on campus: to treat them with the same expectations as any other student; to understand where skin color made a difference, and where it did not.

The Clarence Thomas that Brooks saw that summer was funny, ambitious, relaxed, and in love. His intensity hadn't diminished, but his anger seemed less corrosive and more in check. Gil Hardy, too, had a confidence and disarming sense of humor that Brooks enjoyed. Several months earlier they might have been scared and angry young men willing to abandon their education to stand on principle. But in the summer of 1970 they were two college kids, working and laughing and hanging out with each other, determined to enjoy their freedom before another year at school.

ELEVEN

Eyes on the Prize

President John Brooks surveyed the campus in September 1970 with the eyes of a new leader. He was taking charge of a school with decaying buildings, budget deficits, and a meager endowment. The political and social unrest of the previous year looked likely to continue, and the level of scholarship support, according to his staff in the admissions office, was unsustainable.

Despite the myriad of obstacles he was facing, one of Brooks's first acts was to proceed with his plans to admit female students. Many of his colleagues remained opposed to the idea, which had been rejected by the Board of Trustees a few years earlier. The college had commissioned one report that estimated the cost of coeducation at $2.5 million. In order to fully accommodate women, the report concluded, Holy Cross would have to install a full-length mirror and more closet space in every female's residence room. Brooks scoffed at the idea. One factor in opposing coeducation was how the administration intended to go about it. Rather than simply expand the total student body to accommodate women, as colleges like Amherst and Bowdoin had done, Holy Cross planned to enroll three hundred fewer men in order to keep the total freshman class at the same size. He promised the trustees that the three hundred women would be at least as good, or better, than their male counterparts. He had also personally taken steps to change the balance of trustees in his favor. When a spot came vacant on the board, he would personally interview alumni about their views on admitting women and only put forward candidates who were in favor of the idea. As a result, Brooks knew the proposal would easily pass when he brought it to the board again, and the new president soon announced that the school would admit women for the fall of 1972. "The educational arguments are persuasive," he told a student reporter. They were, in fact, the same arguments he had used in recruiting black students: Any college that wanted to stay relevant and in the top tier had to reach out to every group of future leaders. Ted Wells, Eddie Jenkins, Stan Grayson, and Ed Jones would be among the last students to have an all-male education at Holy Cross.

Clarence Thomas was relieved to be a senior and looked forward to being a resident assistant on the corridor. Along with getting his own room, it meant he could abandon his job as a waiter in the dining hall and he would be paid to dole out advice to other black students. With law school on the horizon, Thomas wanted total freedom to study at any hour without having to worry about disturbing a roommate. He'd made a vow just before the summer to stop putting his future at risk by taking part in the angry and increasingly volatile demonstrations against the war, and he had come back to school in the fall determined to keep it. There was too much at stake.

Another thing had happened over the summer. He had read two books that were to influence his attitude toward life: Ayn Rand's *Atlas Shrugged* and *The Fountainhead*. He had first come across the books in high school, but this time Rand's message of radical individualism and her notion of rational self-interest truly sank in. Thomas agreed with her philosophy that reality was objective and couldn't be changed just because a majority of people wished it were so. To him it helped explain the disconnect he increasingly felt between his views and those of other black students, and the divide between him and his grandfather. "I started to realize that just because I felt alone in my views of certain things didn't mean I was wrong," he recalls. Rand's idea that being productive was man's central purpose and noblest ability also helped Thomas to develop an increasing appreciation for Father Brooks, who had long encouraged him to get beyond his angry musings. It was Brooks who had kept telling him that everything would be fine if he just took faith in his own abilities and worked hard. When Thomas would get angry about the perceived arrogance of the other black students or the assumptions that he believed others were making about his skin color, it was Brooks who would shrug and remind him that it was a fool's mission to try changing anyone in the world but himself. On practically every other matter, from the existence of God to the role of society in helping individuals, John Brooks and Ayn Rand stood apart. But on one matter, they shared a belief: Think for yourself.

Several men on the corridor noticed a change in the senior. Thomas had become less inclined to participate in protests or other forms of activism on campus. He didn't join in the student fast when Marine recruiters returned to campus that fall. While he still spoke up at BSU meetings, there were times when he was content just to sit and listen. It wasn't so much that his views had changed, some members felt, as that he left them with the impression that he no longer really cared. Whatever the BSU was fighting for, it seemed certain that Thomas felt it was no longer fighting on his behalf. He was moving on. He was determined to get a scholarship offer from Harvard or Yale. He planned to marry Kathy Ambush. Yet he hadn't abandoned his ideals, and he talked to Brooks and others about taking a job in the South after getting a law degree, to promote Dr. King's message and help defend civil rights.

As Thomas's confidence had grown, there was less occasion for the two of them to meet. When he had arrived as a sophomore, Thomas had found in Father Brooks a much-needed pillar of support. With all the anger he'd built up from the seminary and the rigid expectations of his grandfather, he hadn't recognized how he was feeling about himself. Beneath the vitriol and the resentment, Brooks saw an obstacle bigger than a label that people might impose on him: his own sense that he was unworthy. Even as he worked twice as hard, laughed twice as loud, and tried to form connections well beyond the confines of the BSU, Thomas would fall back to thinking that he wasn't going to get the grades, the friends, or the respect that seemed to come so easily to others. Brooks had persistently reassured the young man that he was entitled to ask for, and work for, whatever he wanted. While the priest didn't try to downplay the existence of racism, he encouraged Thomas not to go out of his way to look for it or to give it all that much power. There was only so much that could stop a man who pursued excellence, Brooks believed, and he encouraged Thomas to persevere. With the praise from his professors, the warm embrace he'd received from the Ambushes, and the easy friendship he enjoyed with men like Gil Hardy, Thomas had started to believe Brooks's message. By his senior year Thomas knew one thing had changed from where he was two years earlier: He had started to grow up.

Thomas continued to welcome the chance to talk to Father Brooks, but often it would be a smile and a greeting if they ran into each other on campus rather than a long talk in Brooks's office. When they did meet, the conversation was less focused on Thomas's insecurities than it was on his plans, or some issue in the news. Brooks recalled a particular interest that the senior took in Philip and Daniel Berrigan, two Roman Catholic priests and brothers who were in the news for burning draft files as part of the Catonsville Nine. Phil, who had attended Holy Cross with Brooks, was also allegedly leading a plot to blow up Washington steam tunnels and kidnap National Security Advisor Henry Kissinger. The anarchist priest had come to campus in March 1968 to deliver a homily at a Mass, where he spoke against "the U.S. military establishment." Brooks saw the Berrigans as men whose methods might be suspect but whose hearts were clearly devoted to peace and civil rights. When they had gone missing after their convictions for burning draft files, and briefly appeared as outlaws to give sermons before vanishing again, Brooks had silently cheered. He agreed with their views that the Church and, in fact, the leaders of all denominations hadn't done enough to speak out against the senseless slaughter of young lives in Vietnam. Brooks later noted with a hint of wistfulness that one of the FBI agents who picked Dan up by posing as a birdwatcher in August 1970 was a Holy Cross graduate. Thomas was decidedly less sympathetic to the brothers' radical methods than Brooks, who had supported and pushed for a special issue of *Holy Cross Quarterly* to be devoted to the meaning of the Berrigans in January 1971. The notoriety of the Berrigans would land them on the cover of *Time* magazine in January 1971, with a story titled "Rebel Priests: The Curious Case of the Berrigans." (Holy Cross's role in educating men like Berrigan and *The Other America* author Michael Harrington would three years later prompt *Time* to label the college "the cradle of the Catholic Left.")

Both Father Brooks and Clarence Thomas were haunted by the specter of Vietnam. When a student came to Brooks or one of the other Jesuit priests in a panic when his number was called, there was little they could do but recommend that the conscientious objector escape to Canada—even though they knew that meant the draft dodger would be dubbed a traitor and would be unlikely to ever return to the States again. Unlike Eddie Jenkins, Thomas had passed the physical. His draft lottery number was a relatively low 109, but he had managed to defer service at least until he graduated in June. At that point, though, his status would automatically convert to 1-A: ready for immediate induction. Even with the United States cutting back troop numbers in Vietnam, it appeared almost certain that he would be deployed. The idea left him frozen with fear.

Ted Wells was also a resident assistant on the black corridor, and he took on the role of a watchful older brother to the newer students. Students on the corridor would sometimes feel Wells slip an arm around their shoulders and know that a lecture was coming on about a missed English class or a mediocre grade; and if anyone had even the faintest whiff of marijuana on them, they knew to keep Wells at a safe distance. It was one reason, Brooks later concluded, that the black corridor was never a source of complaints or trouble at the school. While drunken rowdiness, fights, or drug use was an issue at other residences from time to time, the black students seemed to demonstrate more discipline. Brooks wasn't sure if that was because they were less interested in getting falling-down drunk or if people like Wells helped to keep things in line. Unlike Clarence Thomas, Wells had never really gone to Brooks to seek comfort. Even when he'd dropped football his freshman year, his goal in seeking out Brooks hadn't been to debate the decision but to check the impact it would have on his scholarship. As Brooks saw it, Wells didn't need a confidence boost, nor did Eddie Jenkins or Stan Grayson. The athletes had either come in with a stronger sense of identity, or they had a well-honed knack for supporting one another. In either case, they typically approached Brooks with a keen understanding of what they or the BSU wanted, and how the president could help.

Ted Wells stepped back from a formal role in running the BSU during the second semester of his junior year to focus on his own goals. He had set his sights on becoming a Fenwick Scholar, one of the highest honors at Holy Cross. Each year a department nominated a third-year student to design an independent research project in lieu of coursework for his senior year; the chosen scholar would then present his findings to the college community at the end of the project. With cable television emerging as a new industry, Wells had become fascinated with the way that cities handled the licensing of new TV franchises. Would they consolidate power in the hands of a few or use cable to democratize the media? For his project Wells proposed creating a primer on the emerging issues that were facing cities and examine how they could be handled. He would do his research, he suggested, while working for the city of Boston's Department of Economic Development. The committee was impressed and promptly chose Wells as the college's first black Fenwick Scholar.

Nina Mitchell was spending almost every weekend with Wells at Holy Cross. While she was thriving as a sociology student at Newton, she had found the move to Boston to be a culture shock. All of a sudden, security officers were following her around stores, and the city's fierce battles over busing had made skin color the only thing some people saw. Worcester, despite its challenges, could feel like an oasis in comparison. But it was a working oasis. Soon after she would arrive on Friday, Mitchell would join Wells at the library, where the two of them would find a spot to study together in the stacks. On Saturdays they would eat breakfast and chat with the men on the corridor before walking back to the library. Sundays were more of the same.

Mitchell marveled at how much her boyfriend had changed since they had left high school. Wells had always cared about his grades, but he had become much more driven at Holy Cross. There was a sense of purpose about him, a willingness to see himself as a leader and to act like one. She admired his commitment to helping the black community —at Holy Cross, and in the world beyond the college. He had far-reaching ambitions, and his dedication was infectious.

The black corridor had moved down a floor to accommodate the larger group of sophomores coming in from the class of '73, recruits who'd lived in freshman dorms the year before. There was a new feeling of vibrancy to the residence, an energy fueled by numbers and a growing sense of black pride. There also was no need to fill out the corridor with white students now, though a few remained because of their strong ties to their black roommates. The men had painted the hallway in the color of the African Liberation Flag—red, black, and green. The energy level increased as the men new to the corridor seemed less inclined to camp at the library than hang out, listening to James Brown or Sly & the Family Stone. Whether it was Joe Wilson dancing with layers of gold chains around his neck in an impression of soul singer Isaac Hayes, or Gil Hardy cracking jokes, the men kept one another entertained. Ma Wells often visited, serving up the soul food that she now personally delivered in periodic visits to Worcester. In recalling the barbs, the jokes, and the camaraderie, several men compared that time to their version of a fraternity—though a fraternity where even mild debauchery took a clear backseat to getting the work done, especially when Wells was around.

The Black Muslim students who had arrived as freshmen the year before were no longer just new voices at the BSU meetings but a force on the corridor. When not working on their coursework the men could be found circulating copies of *Muhammad Speaks* or practicing martial arts. While many of the others admired their discipline, they also enjoyed poking fun at their zeal, and the Muslim students sometimes took similar delight in ribbing the men for not following the ways of Elijah

Muhammad and Malcolm X. Wells, for one, would brace himself in the cafeteria when a Muslim hallmate walked by and looked at his food. "Now, brother, you ain't eating that pig, are you?" he would ask Wells in mock disdain. Wells would then look down at his meal with raised eyebrows. "Is that pork, brother?" he would respond, pushing the offending meat aside. "No sir, brother. No way am I eating that."

Eddie Jenkins enjoyed spending time with the Muslim students. While he found them more serious than the other black students—nobody would have ever dared to joke about Louis Farrakhan in their presence—he also discovered that many of them had interesting views on politics and what was happening in the rest of the world. They were well informed and passionate, so much so that Jenkins found himself drifting into their circle. He had even taken to reading the Koran a bit, occasionally joining their trips to the Boston mosque. In addition, he loved the food that the Muslim students prepared: the salmon mixed with mayonnaise and apples or raisins, the brussel sprouts with hot sauce, the bean pies, fresh whole wheat bread, red peppers, and olives.

As president, Brooks made it a point to visit most of the residences, usually at the invitation of the students, though his office would sometimes reach out and solicit an offer. Typically he would chat for a few minutes about what was going on at the college and then take questions. In his frequent visits to the corridor, though, he sometimes started by asking the men questions. He continued to take an interest in BSU issues that could have been handed on to someone else, now that he was college president. When the BSU van broke down on the Massachusetts Turnpike and the director of purchasing argued that it shouldn't be replaced, Brooks personally ordered a new twelve-passenger van for the BSU at a cost of $3,670.

Some colleagues continued to think that Brooks took too direct an interest in the students. Having fought so hard to bring them back to campus, the president now seemed focused on doing whatever it took to keep them there. It wasn't so much racism or even the isolation that drove some men to quit or transfer, he suspected, but self-esteem. Although they may have arrived as class valedictorians and A students, a few of the men simply didn't believe they could keep up. The result was that they didn't, and that made them isolate themselves even further from campus life. Brooks tried to encourage them to ignore their fears and do the work. But one thing he didn't intervene in was grades.

It was clear that the obstinate and sometimes high-handed approach Father Brooks took as dean wasn't going to change now that he had the top job. He spent a lot of time talking to professors, but even he had to admit that he rarely asked them for approval or input. He believed in acting on his own beliefs, without getting bogged down in unnecessary debate. What Holy Cross needed most was money: Having slipped to around $4 million, the school's endowment was too low to be of any real use. Brooks wanted to upgrade the buildings and maintenance of the grounds, and he wanted to bring in more students on scholarship, but none of that was possible without money. The problem wasn't that Holy Cross alumni weren't loyal, he'd decided, it was that they hadn't been asked to give. One of his immediate priorities as president was to visit alumni across the United States and around the world and simply ask them to give more money to the college. In the meantime, though, there were even harder choices to make. *The Crusader* published articles stating that Holy Cross might be forced to turn away working-class students who couldn't afford to pay the tuition. School officials talked about the need for the school to draw on state aid. Brooks personally assured Ted Wells that he didn't want to cut back on aid to black students, but it would be a strain. The lingering anger of some alumni over the walkout meant that talking about the need to recruit more black students might not yield the best response. Everyone had to be realistic, especially the members of the BSU.

Sophomore Henry De Bernardo, the new head of the union, was pushing for a radical increase in black student enrollment. This time Brooks said it wasn't feasible. "I am very much aware of the amount of time and effort you and your brothers put into the drafting of this proposal," Brooks wrote to De Bernardo. "As you might well expect, Henry, my main objection, and it is a major one, is the unrealistic and absolutely impossible obligation to which the proposal would commit the

College." Holy Cross was in its third year of deficit spending and had already committed to give out more than $1.5 million in aid. Regardless of whether he could raise more funds from alumni, Brooks was determined to balance the school's budget.

Father Brooks had already decided that football was a place to tighten the belt. It turned out to be a good time to question the merits of big-time football. The 1970 season opened with a 26–0 loss against West Point. The hepatitis outbreak had robbed the Crusaders of experience, and it showed. And though Coach Bill Whitton was determined to make a comeback, it didn't look likely. Early in the year, Eddie Jenkins was heralded in *The Crusader* as having "all the tools for stardom," and the much-lauded Joe Wilson was now a starter on the team. As Whitton said to reporters in September, the goal was to show everyone that "Holy Cross football is improving, getting better all the time."

Still, in the second game the Crusaders lost to Temple, 23–13, and at their game against Boston University in October, Jenkins caught a 99-yard touchdown pass, tying an NCAA record, but the Crusaders still lost, 33–23.

In November a plane carrying the Marshall University football team crashed in West Virginia, killing everyone on board, and the Crusaders dedicated their season to Marshall. Midway through the season, Jenkins broke his arm and had to sit out the final four games. The high point for the team came with a 20–20 tie against Connecticut. The varsity football team from Holy Cross simply couldn't compete. Jaffe Dickerson decided to quit the team. Standing in the mud and rain at one practice, convinced that Whitton already hated him, Dickerson turned to Jenkins and said, "This is it, man. I've had enough." Jenkins made a halfhearted attempt to talk him out of it, but he could see the frustration in his friend's eyes. No one on the coaching staff tried to talk Dickerson into staying.

Morale had hit an all-time low, and many were unhappy with Whitton. The goodwill he had enjoyed in the aftermath of the Tom Boisture era was gone. The assistant coaches complained that Whitton's behavior was erratic and that his drinking had become more frequent. The players, defeated by their string of losses, weren't inclined to support their coach.

The final game of the season was the always-popular battle against Boston College. Most of the men were feeling down the morning of the game. They ate breakfast together and one player jokingly referred to the meal as "the Last Supper." When several players began discussing their lousy odds against the strong Boston team, Whitton exploded. The team had no drive, he screamed. They had no passion. Did they even know what the Holy Cross players of 1942 had achieved when they'd trounced the then-undefeated Boston College team? They had pulled off one of the greatest upsets in college history. Why couldn't the men on this team be more like that one? Why couldn't they win just one damn game when it mattered?

If Whitton had intended to motivate his team, he failed. On the bus to Boston College, some players started grumbling. "I'm not playing for that guy," one said. "Who does he think he is?" A demoralized squad ran onto the field and ended up getting crushed, 54–0. Jenkins saw his future slipping away. It had been more than two years since the team had won a game. He wondered if the team's setbacks were too serious to recover from. He also began to fear that his next season would be a swan song for his football career.

While Father Brooks was pondering how to deal with an elaborate football infrastructure that no longer suited the school's needs, the more immediate issue was Whitton. At Brooks's prompting, the coach resigned in February 1971, citing his health and family concerns. "I leave with no ill feeling to Father Brooks, the athletic department or the college," Whitton told *The Crusader.*

Though the basketball team was doing much better than the football team, winning nine of its first eleven games in 1970, Stan Grayson was having frustrations of his own. Despite averaging 21 points a game as a freshman offensive player, Coach Donohue had decided to switch him to a defensive role. The junior could tell that he was no longer playing to his strengths, but he worked hard to make up for it. Unlike some other players, who openly balked at Donohue's style of coaching, Grayson didn't complain. It wasn't his style. *The Crusader* called him the most underrated performer on the team, noting that he managed to average 11.2 points and 10 rebounds a game even though he was consistently paired off against the opposition's top scorer. Grayson became known as a defensive workhorse, forcing opposing stars who normally racked up 20 or 25 points a game to average fewer than 12 points when he was guarding them.

Grayson's most daunting assignment that season was covering a University of Massachusetts junior named Julius Erving. The Crusaders stood at 11 wins and 5 losses when they faced off against the UMass team in Worcester. When Grayson held Erving to two hoops in the first half, the crowd started to sing "Sweet Swingin' Stan." The Crusaders were leading 27–26 when Grayson was called on two quick fouls—his third and fourth of the game—and Donohue had to pull him out. In Grayson's six minutes off the court, Erving scored 12 points. By the time Grayson got back into the game, it was too late. The Crusaders lost by two points, 60–58, and Erving scored 32 points and pulled down 17 rebounds. Donohue told a Holy Cross reporter that "Stan was great. Unfortunately, Julius Erving was just a bit better."

Grayson had increasingly expanded his focus to pursuits other than basketball. He was still dating Vicki Mitchell, Nina's sister. He joined the 1843 Club to help organize concerts on campus, which meant he would get good seats to shows and have some say over who played at Holy Cross, from the Fifth Dimension to Smokey Robinson and the Miracles. One of club's coups was getting the band Chicago to play at a bargain price by booking them just before their debut album became a hit. Grayson had to help defuse a near riot when the number of people with tickets was double the number that had been sold. The club had issued black-and-white tickets that could be—and were—easily photocopied.

Ed Jones just wanted to write. After doing well in Maurice Geracht's Nineteenth-Century Novel class, he had enrolled in the college's first creative writing course. The class was small, about ten people, and its focus was on reading celebrated short stories in order to understand their structure; then the students would imitate the style of the writers. Geracht was impressed not only with Jones's ability to stay ahead in the readings but with his ability to adapt his own writing to closely match writers ranging from Charles Dickens to Henry James. Geracht also praised Jones for having a strong voice of his own in his stories, as well as a sensitivity to the characters he chronicled. "It was then that I knew I had talent," Jones later recalled. He liked the sparse discipline of the short story, the chance to paint textured vignettes and breathe life into the kind of characters who might otherwise disappear in the margins of some epic tale. About twenty years later, that passion was evident when he published his first book, *Lost in the City*, a collection of poignant short stories about black men and women in Washington, D.C.

Jones wasn't surprised when Clarence Thomas was accepted to both Harvard and Yale law schools: Thomas had made his aspirations known for some time, telling Gil Hardy that he was tired of being poor. On a trip that Jones, Thomas, Hardy, Ted Wells, and Eddie Jenkins had taken to a conference for potential law students at New York's Fordham University the year they arrived at Holy Cross, Jones was struck by Clarence's persistence in gathering material and quizzing the folks from Yale about what it would take to get in. On the drive back to Worcester, Ted Wells was sleeping on Jones's shoulder and everyone was battling exhaustion, but Thomas, who was behind the wheel, refused to pull over to rest. Instead he stopped six times to buy coffee to keep himself awake. "He was determined to get into Yale," Jones recalled. "In everything he did, Clarence was determined."

Thomas received the acceptance letter from Harvard first. When he called his grandmother with the good news, she seemed unimpressed. "That's nice, son, if that's what you want to do," she told him. "But when you going to stop going to school?" His grandfather wouldn't even come to the phone. When he received that acceptance from Yale, he didn't call home. At the time, he assumed that his grandparents either didn't understand the importance of getting into an Ivy League school, or they didn't care. In their world, men worked hard with their hands from dawn to dusk and made a living for their families if they weren't going to devote themselves to God. Men didn't stay in school for years, reading books. He would later discover that his grandfather did care and was deeply proud of his grandson's accomplishments. The signs were small—his grandfather displayed Holy Cross and Yale bumper stickers on his 1968 Pontiac, and one day when a man asked him why he was driving around with stickers he didn't deserve, he proudly retorted that his grandson had graduated with honors from those schools. When Myers Anderson told Thomas the story, Thomas choked up with emotion.

In the waning weeks of his senior year, Thomas felt a fresh connection to the men on the corridor. After rereading Richard Wright's *Native Son* and Ralph Ellison's *Invisible Man* in his last semester, he felt a renewed appreciation for the sense of fraternity that he had built with the men on the corridor. Years later he would reflect fondly on the living arrangement. "We laughed. We teased each other. There could be a real party atmosphere at times. I had no enemies there; we were all good brothers. We worked hard, and we respected each other, even when we didn't agree. I have all the time in the world for those men. It was a special time in my life."

As graduation neared, Thomas was especially sad to say goodbye to Father Brooks. Brooks had supported Thomas for three years, helping him express his anger and refine his personal beliefs. More important, Thomas felt that Father Brooks had treated him as an individual, one with anxieties and strengths that had nothing to do with being black. To Thomas the priest was a combination of friend, uncle, priest, father, saint, and Good Samaritan. "He was the one who inspired me there," Thomas would later say. "You always felt he had your best interests at heart; I wasn't part of some program to Father Brooks. I was a kid. I was an honors student and I didn't complain, but I was a kid who found it hard to go to a white college in Worcester, Massachusetts. Somehow, he understood that, and thank God he did. Holy Cross was content to educate me and let me do my own thing. Father Brooks tried to help us, but he never tried to work any issues out through us. He wanted the college to have more black students because it was the right thing to do; it was the right thing for us as individuals. We weren't symbols to him. We were just kids."

Clarence Thomas graduated ninth in his class—cum laude—with a degree in English. A day later, on June 5, 1971, he married Kathy Ambush at All Saints Episcopal Church in Worcester. Gil Hardy was his best man. The couple moved into an efficiency apartment in New Haven, Connecticut, where Thomas prepared to attend Yale. That September, Thomas had a medical exam for entry into the service. This time the doctors found a curvature in his spine, and he failed. He wouldn't have to go to Vietnam after all.

New Haven turned out to be a miserable experience for Thomas. Yale's law school had an aggressive affirmative action program, and Thomas felt the sting of low expectations every day he was there. He wanted the college to believe he could do anything, that he was as smart and deserving as every other student in his class. At Yale, he realized how much Brooks had given him. For all the angst and isolation he had privately felt during his years in Worcester, not once in his three years there had Thomas doubted his own intelligence.

TWELVE

Moving On

The ten black seniors returning to Holy Cross in the fall of 1971—all who were left of the original nineteen—felt a mix of excitement and urgency. All the hours of studying, debating, laughing, all the moments of frustration, confidence, and doubt had to lead somewhere. Eddie Jenkins let out a whoop when he saw sophomore Ron Lawson move onto the corridor with a color TV. Within weeks, he and Joe Wilson were kicking the young man out of his room on the nights that they wanted to watch football. The two of them would stand at the sophomore's door with snacks and drinks in hand. "You need to study, man! Get to the library," they'd say.

That September, Jenkins savored a 21–16 victory over Harvard's football team. It had been 1,036 days since the Holy Cross varsity team had won a game, and the win stunned everyone. *The New York Times* praised Jenkins and Wilson for their skills and "gung ho attitude." At the end of the game, the crowd had cheered as the Crusaders hoisted Coach Ed Doherty on their shoulders and carried him off the Harvard field. Holy Cross students rushed out of the stands to lift some of the players onto their shoulders, too.

With graduation looming, Jenkins found himself thinking more about his future. Law school seemed like a logical option, and he began to hunt for schools. He hadn't spent his weekends buried in books at the library, but he had worked hard enough during the week to earn decent grades. He had been thinking about the possibility of playing football professionally. He'd have to distinguish himself on the field and hope that the team could win enough games to draw some attention.

As co-captain of the basketball team, Stan Grayson also began his senior year with high hopes. The team had done well the year before, with 18 wins and 8 losses, but most of their losses had been in the season's final games, when the stakes were highest. Grayson was confident that the team could do better this year. He was feeling more assertive; he had even challenged Coach Donohue on his strict policy prohibiting facial hair and won the right to sport a well-trimmed mustache.

Ted Wells was living on the corridor again, now as a resident assistant, along with Grayson, but he was feeling less interested in the campus goings-on. As a Fenwick Scholar he was exempt from classes for the year. Instead he commuted to Boston a few days a week to immerse himself in the nascent cable industry. He found himself fascinated by how entrepreneurs were trying to build a business model around the new networks. While he was still committed to law school, he was increasingly drawn to the business world and was starting to think about a way to combine his two interests.

Father Brooks had helped nominate Wells for a Rhodes scholarship, one of the most lucrative and coveted international scholarships, which provided funding for two years of study at England's Oxford University. Though Wells was conflicted about the scholarship, he decided to go for it. He told another student on the corridor that he wanted to get the scholarship so that he could turn it down. It bothered him intensely that the most prestigious postgraduate scholarship in the country honored the memory of Cecil Rhodes, someone he considered to be the worst of the European colonists. Rhodes had openly declared that British-born whites—the Anglo-Saxons—were the finest race in the world. He had colonized large tracts of southern Africa and exploited the region when he founded the diamond company De Beers. It gave Wells immense satisfaction to think that if he got the scholarship, he might have an opportunity to draw attention to its racist history.

Wells decided to apply out of his home region rather than New England, and when he went down to Baltimore for the final set of interviews at Johns Hopkins University, he began to have doubts about his plan. After speaking with other candidates, he could see clearly how much the award meant to them. They just wanted to study at Oxford. By the time Wells was called into the interview room, his resolve had left him. Having loudly proclaimed his intent to turn the scholarship down, Wells found himself giving lackluster answers to the interviewer, a young politician named Paul Sarbanes. In the end the scholarship was awarded to someone else. Wells later found out that the committee had awarded it to a black man, Kurt Schmoke, a year earlier. Schmoke went on to become the mayor of Baltimore, a state attorney, and dean of the Howard University School of Law, as well as a close friend of Wells.

Wells was looking forward to marrying Nina Mitchell. He had asked her to marry him the previous spring, having already "pinned" her with the purple-jeweled Holy Cross pin. Though they'd planned to marry after graduation, Wells now wanted to hold the wedding over the Christmas break. He argued that they didn't have enough money for a big ceremony in any case, and he didn't understand why they needed to wait. Their families had been getting together for Christmas dinners every year, so he suggested that it would be economical to turn the 1971 dinner into their wedding reception. And one benefit of the otherwise lackluster Rhodes interview experience was that it had allowed Wells to pick up the appropriate paperwork for a marriage certificate in Washington.

Mitchell didn't mind; she hadn't been interested in planning a big wedding. A few weeks before Christmas she went down to the "Hit or Miss" store near Newton College and bought a red dress for fifteen dollars. Wells borrowed a colorful dashiki from a friend on the corridor. He and Mitchell were married in the late afternoon on December 25, 1971, with Stan Grayson and a few other friends on hand to witness the event. The reception was a turkey dinner at Mitchell's mother's house. Wells calculated that the entire affair couldn't have cost more than fifty dollars.

For his last semester, Wells moved off campus to an apartment in

Ted Wells and Nina Mitchell at their wedding

Boston with Mitchell. He had set his sights on a new program at Harvard University—one that offered a joint law degree and a master of business administration. He had briefly considered pursuing a doctorate in economics but abandoned the idea because he had no interest in an academic career. A Holy Cross trustee and federal judge, John Gibbons, had offered to write him a recommendation for Harvard on the condition that he consider interning for him when he finished law school, and Wells had agreed.

Meanwhile, faculty and student outrage over the black corridor continued to be an issue, with some arguing to Brooks that it was hypocritical to condemn racial segregation in one place, only to tolerate it somewhere else. Brooks openly admitted that he never liked the idea of the corridor, but found himself in the uncomfortable position of having to defend it. Nevertheless, he stood firm, noting that every resident had made his own decision to live there. Ed Jones, for one, didn't understand the continued fuss. Every other dorm on campus was just a dorm until he or another black student stepped inside it; then it became a dorm of white people. It was his campus, too, but Jones felt like a visitor on it much of the time. He liked the sense of brotherhood on the corridor, the feeling that he could depend on the guys there. Nobody ever talked about it, but it felt like home.

There were times when the expectations ran too high, though. By Eddie Jenkins's final year, he and five Muslims would prepare their own meals on the corridor with special food deliveries authorized by Brooks. With raised eyes and the occasional exasperated sigh, the Kimball staff would hand the men cases of honey, navy beans, frozen okra, asparagus tips, and other vegetables. They had to purchase a vast range of fish, including smoked herring, lake trout, red snapper, and the ubiquitous cans of salmon. The Kimball staff even ordered boxes of a special herbal tea for the men. Brooks fielded complaints that that the men were consuming too much juice—complaints that the Muslim students called "petty and characteristically racist"—and played down the issues in his responses. Nobody was going to quit school or their jobs over juice.

Brooks was facing a growing tide of discontent on campus. The protests against the war continued, and he couldn't always be there to help calm things down. At a protest against a visit by Marine recruiters, Brooks was too ill to show up and monitor the situation. The crowd of angry students grew in strength, demanding to speak with Brooks, only to be told that the president was sick. Some of the students then tried to pull down a light pole. From his bed in the Jesuit residence, Brooks directed that a second day of Marine recruitment be postponed. Four students were brought before the College Judicial Board. This time all were found not guilty.

School officials appeared to be extra cautious about whom they charged. While several black students were involved in the demonstration, none was brought before the board. At another Marine visit in the spring, Brooks even agreed to join in a demonstration as long as the protesters wouldn't prevent fellow students from meeting with recruiters. Brooks hoped to promote an open dialogue on Vietnam by holding the protest without disturbing the recruitment drive. It was an ambitious aim. Before the event, though, someone called the college switchboard to say that a bomb would explode between 12:45 and 1:00 P.M. at the site. Brooks didn't want to take any chances, so everyone was cleared out. A few days earlier a vandal had tossed two firebombs in the window of the Air Force ROTC building, causing smoke and other damage. This time, however, no bomb was found.

Despite the chaotic atmosphere on campus, Brooks refused to cancel classes. He was tired of a handful of protesters disrupting everyone else's education. He issued a statement stressing the college's "legal and moral obligation" to the students. "It's your choice whether you want your feelings about the war to disrupt your education," wrote Brooks. "Personally, I feel we can make our feelings known without harming our own futures." A planned campus-wide strike failed when more than three-quarters of students continued attending class.

On May 3, about eighty black students—the bulk of the BSU—took over the Fenwick-O'Kane complex, two buildings that housed administrative offices. The goal was to highlight their continued demands for black faculty, courses, and other accommodations on campus. Eddie Jenkins, Ed Jones, and Gordon Davis were among the students who snuck into the building at 1:45 A.M., carrying knapsacks, food, rope, and wire. The BSU had been talking about doing something to put black issues back on the college agenda, and it seemed there was a need for a dramatic statement if they wanted to get attention amid the other protests. They weren't particularly worried about repercussions. The walkout had made it clear that there was safety in numbers, and Holy Cross had taken the stance that the black students were too important to kick out en masse.

The students planned to take over the complex and hold a press conference after everyone on campus woke up. They expected that their sympathizers would bring them meals but, just in case, they had stocked up on drinks and snacks. As they wandered through the complex, they stationed a few members at every entrance door. But in the ROTC offices of the building, they ran into a group of twenty-five white students staging a sit-in to protest the war. The students told the BSU protesters that they were not leaving until Holy Cross agreed to stop all military recruiting, training, and contracts by September. It seemed like a bad joke to Jenkins. He had no problem with an antiwar protest, but the last thing the black students needed was a group of white hippies getting in the way as they tried to occupy a building.

The two sides stood arguing. It was too late to go looking for another building to take over, and in any case, a residence building would hardly have the same impact. The two groups finally agreed that the white activists could stay in the ROTC offices, as long as they didn't go anywhere else in the building, or muscle into the black students' press conference with their own list of demands.

Father Brooks heard about the takeover as soon as he woke up. He couldn't help but think that if Ted Wells had been head of the BSU, rather than Henry De Bernardo, the group might have come up with a different strategy. But Ted, now living in Boston, hadn't been consulted. He arrived at the front door of O'Kane at 8 A.M. and found Ogretta McNeil trying to deal with the protesters. One of the black students stopped Brooks at the door to tell him that they would be holding a press conference at 10 A.M. to state their position. When Brooks asked him if the takeover was really necessary, the student shrugged.

At 10 A.M., Eddie Jenkins read a BSU statement to the three hundred students, reporters, and onlookers who were gathered on the steps. "The black community at Holy Cross College has been victimized by the racist tentacles that ensnarl the larger black community in America," he read. "Increasingly, the administration of this institution has been nonchalant and apathetic to the needs and aspirations of its black community." He went on to list the students' grievances, including accusations that the director of financial aid had a negative attitude toward black students, charges of discrimination against black workers at Kimball, inadequate efforts to design a black studies program, and an indifferent attitude toward rewarding BSU efforts to recruit black students. They also believed that the college's investment in General Tire & Rubber, which had a production facility in South Africa, demonstrated that Holy Cross had "no regard for the welfare of black people." In summary, the BSU members stated, "we refuse to be written off as mere entities used by this administration to ostensibly cover up its true racist, apathetic nature. We demand to be recognized as viable, positive forces on this campus, and in accordance we will fight with every means available to us to see that we are given that respect we deserve."

Bypassing the white ROTC protesters, Brooks and McNeil headed inside to talk to Henry De Bernardo. Brooks knew the young man was upset about the lack of funding to support a bigger expansion in black recruitment, but he hadn't imagined the students would resort to commandeering campus facilities. Over the next several hours, Brooks reiterated that they were trying to bring in more black professors and staff, and as many qualified black students as the budget would allow. And, said Brooks, they would review stock holdings and discrimination claims. He explained that he and the BSU didn't have any major differences of opinion in this area.

That afternoon, Brooks stood on the front steps of the complex to read his own statement, saying that he had "genuine regret" that the black students "thought it necessary to disrupt the normal operations of the college. As president, I fully intend to ensure that all allegations are investigated. At the same time, I retain full faith in the competence and integrity of the individuals involved." The president then invited several of the students to speak with trustees over the weekend. He told the men that he couldn't snap his fingers and instantly diversify the faculty any more than he could instantly eliminate racism or expand financial aid. None of the students, Brooks said, would face disciplinary action because of the protest.

After hearing the president's statement, the protesters voted by a slim margin to leave the building peacefully. As the numbers of spectators dwindled, De Bernardo made it known that the fight wasn't over. One of Brooks's colleagues later joked to the president that the alumni were planning to stage a protest to accuse the president of being anti-white.

When not participating in demonstrations himself, Ed Jones took to chronicling many of the goings-on about campus in his column in *The Crusader*. He remained a quiet enigma to the men on the corridor—quiet in person and yet fierce in print. While he may have felt a strong sense of brotherhood with the other men, he rarely let them know it.

Jones's views came through in his work. He wrote of a tall, thin, bespectacled man who became the sole protector of the ROTC building during one demonstration, bending down to gently cup a dog's head in his hands while demonstrators stomped around him. He described priests screaming at students instead of praying their "helpless rosary beads," as well as middle-class youths aroused to only a fleeting anger before settling back to old routines. In another column, he wrote of "the system of American life where the average white child is brought up hating any color save his own, where whites overly squash black life in every sphere of interaction. Into this hostility is born the black child, soon made to think of himself as inferior."

Jones's mother was sick. She'd had several strokes by his senior year, and it was clear that she was ailing. He wanted to pursue graduate studies and find a way to keep writing, but he needed a job. He thought he would probably head to Washington to look for one—if he didn't get sent to Vietnam first. That was just the way things were. His mother had taught him that dreams set you up for disappointment.

In late January 1972, Stan Grayson was in the second half of a game against Georgetown, having racked up 14 points, when he fell on his left knee. It started to swell as soon as he stood up. He knew in his heart that his basketball career was over. He later discovered that the kneecap was fractured and his anterior cruciate ligament was torn. Without him, the Crusaders lost 6 of their last 10 games.

Grayson was crushed. He had hoped to play professionally for a season or two. Now he would never reach what had seemed like an attainable goal of scoring 1,000 points in his three years on the team. Eddie Jenkins tried to console him by pointing out that his broken arm and ribs proved to be only temporary setbacks in his game, but they both knew that Stan's career as an athlete was over. The basketball star had been approached by football scouts from the New England Patriots, who had been impressed by his size and agility, but now, after the injury, they sent him flowers and a letter saying that he had always been a long shot.

Father Brooks attended every basketball game he could and had always made a point of complimenting Grayson on his play. After the accident, he called Grayson to his office. As Grayson walked in with his bandaged knee, Brooks could see an uncharacteristic air of sadness in the senior's eyes. There was one thing he immediately wanted the senior to understand: "You know, Stanley, you're not here because you play basketball."

Brooks's words gave Grayson great comfort. They talked about what else he was hoping to do with his life. His sights were now set on getting to law school or pursuing a career in education. Brooks offered to write him a recommendation to whichever school he was interested in attending and suggested that he turn up the heat on his studies.

In April Grayson was named "Crusader of the Year"—an award given to a student who excelled not only in sports but also in the classroom and in campus affairs. An article in *The Crusader* argued that Grayson "may be the most popular student on the Holy Cross campus and one of the finest basketball players in the East." Coach Donohue mentioned that Grayson was the first black captain of a major sport at Holy Cross. "But the best thing I can say," he added," is that I have two young sons at home and I hope, sincerely hope, they grow up to be the man Stan Grayson is."

Eddie Jenkins was battling his own doubts about an athletic career. Between injuries and hepatitis, he had played perhaps twenty games over his entire four years at Holy Cross. It seemed unlikely that National Football League teams would even bother to approach him. But after practice one day Coach Doherty told Jenkins and his teammate Bill Adams that some scouts had expressed interest in seeing the two of them. NFL officials arrived shortly thereafter to weigh the seniors and test their skills and conditioning in everything from leaping to bench pressing.

Soon after, Adams was drafted by the Buffalo Bills, but Jenkins hadn't received any news. The wait was killing him. The other men on the corridor were merciless in teasing him. Any time the one pay phone on the corridor would ring, someone would yell "Jenks, it's the NFL on the line," or take the call and insist that it was any number of NFL coaches. One claimed to have told Coach Weeb Ewbank of the New York Jets that Jenkins wasn't available because he was busy "smoking some weed." One evening another call came. "Jenks, some guy from the NFL!"

Jenkins grabbed the phone. The antics were starting to wear on him. "It's Jenks."

"Eddie Jenkins? This is Don Shula speaking."

"Yeah, right, man. Who put you up to this?"

The man sounded confused. "I'm sorry?"

Jenkins paused. The man didn't sound like anyone he knew from Holy Cross. "Who'd you say you were?"

"My name is Don Shula. I'm coach of the Miami Dolphins. We would like to invite you to be part of our team."

"Seriously, this isn't a joke?"

Some of the other men started to gather around the phone. They were quiet as Jenkins listened to the voice on the other end. When he hung up, Jenkins let out a whoop. He had just been drafted onto a team that had made it to the 1971 Super Bowl. He was an eleventh-round pick, but he was thrilled that he would get at least one season in the NFL. His plans to attend Suffolk Law School would have to be put on hold.

Father Brooks was pleased when Jenkins told him the news. "Now, what are we going to do with this, Eddie?" asked the priest. Jenkins was in for a wild ride, Brooks suspected, but he advised the young player to save his money and keep his eye on a career after football. His message was clear: A Holy Cross degree could pay off again down the road.

At the other end of the corridor, Ed Jones quietly packed his bag. He was leaving with little more than he had brought in terms of possessions. Having graduated 150th out of a class of 500, he wasn't going to receive any special accolades. But Jones still felt relatively happy. He had made some good friends in Gordon Davis and Gil Hardy. For the first time in his life, he'd stayed in one place long enough to form some bonds. Mostly he thought about his mother, the one who "could have done so much more in a better world," as he wrote in the dedication of his Pulitzer Prize–winning novel, *The Known World*. On the day of the graduation ceremony, his mother arrived at Holy Cross for the first time, and as Jeanette M. Jones caught a glimpse of the college's brick spires, she burst into tears. Her son had made it through college.

Four years after they had arrived, the men stood together on Mount St. James for their graduation ceremony. Many of their fellow recruits hadn't made it. For the men who had persevered, it was a moment of intense pride.

When Father Brooks saw Eddie Jenkins's outfit at the ceremony, he had to laugh. In accordance with his flamboyant personality, Jenkins was wearing a colorful dashiki to the ceremony as a substitute for the traditional cloak and gown. Jenkins obviously couldn't resist one last chance to make a statement. Brooks wished him luck in the big leagues. Ted Wells was going to Harvard on full scholarship, while Stan Grayson had been admitted to the University of Michigan to study law.

That year the BSU produced a literary magazine called *Black Thing*, which included a statement from Father Brooks. "I can honestly say that

Stan Grayson, Eddie Jenkins, Ted Wells, and Jaffe Dickerson at graduation

I have learned much in the last decade from Richard Wright, James Baldwin, Malcolm X, Eldridge Cleaver, Martin Luther King, Ralph Abernathy, and others," the president wrote. "But I have learned much more from our own Holy Cross black students: for they are my fellow learners in this community of learning which is Holy Cross."

While the class of 1972 was leaving the college behind, Brooks's role as president was just beginning. By the time he stepped down as president more than two decades later, he had balanced twenty-three budgets, successfully transitioned the college to coeducation, and mentored several generations of black students. But he never lost his ties to those men who had arrived in the fall of 1968 and had become leaders in law, literature, and finance. He presided over their weddings and over the funerals of Gil Hardy, who died in a diving accident at the age of thirty-eight, and the toddler daughter of Malcolm Joseph. When Clarence Thomas needed support during his acrimonious confirmation hearings in 1991, Brooks drove down to Washington to testify that the Supreme Court nominee was "a man of compassion, good judgment, and intelligence," with a "zeal for justice, freedom, and equal opportunity for all Americans." He often called the men to say how proud he was of their accomplishments and how sad he felt for their losses. And ultimately he asked many of them back to the college, to serve as trustees and speakers and role models for the next generation of leaders. In 1980, Ted Wells, at the invitation of Father Brooks, would become the first African American to serve as a trustee of Holy Cross. Two years later Clarence Thomas would join Wells as a trustee, and the two of them would serve together for almost a decade. Stan Grayson would also later serve on the board.

Years later Brooks discounted his own role in helping shape and inspire the group. Much of it was God's providence, he said, noting that he could not have succeeded in any of his roles without the presence of God in his life every day. And he felt that he had learned as much from the young recruits as they had learned from him. They had carried the burden of expectations—high and low, their own and others—with grace, humor, and courage. The debt, he insisted, was one that he owed to them. "These men took the risks, not me," he said, looking out at the campus from his office. "They were the pioneers. They did the work. They took a chance on us."

In the spring of 2008, more than four decades after they had enrolled at Holy Cross, Ted Wells and Clarence Thomas stood together outside the hall where they had once protested against an administration that was now welcoming them back with open arms. The campus that had seemed so white to a handful of black men in the 1960s was now home to student groups dealing with issues ranging from eating disorders to the exploration of multicultural identity. The world had changed. Wells put his arms around the shoulders of his old debating foe as they stood together, looking at photos from their Black Student Union days. It was the fortieth anniversary of the founding of the BSU, and the first time that the group of men, whom Father John Brooks had largely recruited, was gathering at the school since graduation.

The current BSU members entertained the roomful of alumni by staging a debate. One young African American turned to the audience and, with emotion in his voice, talked about how affirmative action was undermining progress and made the rest of the world believe that minorities couldn't succeed without special help. The other young man shook his head. Without a process to gain entry to an exclusive and typically homogeneous club—be it a university or some other institution—the club would remain just that: exclusive.

It was about getting the opportunity to compete, not about being handed a prize.

It was a valid debate, if hardly an unfamiliar one. The scene could have taken place four decades earlier and, in fact, it often had. But neither Wells nor Thomas was in the room to witness it. Just before the two students stood up to present their sides of the argument to attendees, Wells had walked over to Thomas and invited him to head out into the hall. The gesture was meant to allow Thomas to avoid any embarrassment, since Thomas had famously devoted much of his career to speaking out against affirmative action. After receiving a full scholarship to Holy Cross, he went on to reject the belief that any ethnic minority should have the same opportunities that he had received. He didn't see his life as a testament to the benefits of affirmative action; he saw it as an example of its perils. He felt that instead of being praised for what he had accomplished when given the opportunity, the fact that he had been given an opportunity because of his skin color had overshadowed the accomplishments. It had negated the hard work and the intelligence necessary to capitalize on whatever breaks he'd had.

Wells, on the other hand, had maintained a strong commitment to helping African Americans rise educationally and professionally, in part through affirmative action and diversity programs. He had served as chairman of the board of the NAACP Legal Defense Fund, the iconic public interest law firm that had litigated the *Brown v. Board of Education* case. In fact, the two had come in direct opposition with each other in another Supreme Court case: the 2003 decision that narrowly upheld the Univeristy of Michigan Law School's affirmative action program. Wells had personally filed the amicus brief on behalf of law students at Harvard, Yale, and Stanford; Thomas had written the dissenting opinion. And yet, that day, as an auditorium full of their old roommates and fellow alumni listened to the arguments that Wells and Thomas had once used against each other, the two stood arm in arm in the hall, laughing at old photos taped to a bulletin board.

Neither of them wanted to talk about their differences anymore.

Long ago the two men had reached an unspoken understanding: they simply did not discuss their different views concerning the merits of affirmative action, how the U.S. Constitution should be interpreted or the philosophies that had made Wells a liberal Democrat and Thomas a conservative Republican. What they shared now was their love of Father Brooks and their shared experiences at Holy Cross. They came to the reunion to laugh about their old Afros and to connect with their brothers. Most important, they were there to honor Father John Brooks. Now slightly stooped at the age of eighty-four, Brooks was president emeritus of the college—one of the most revered and longest-serving presidents in the history of Holy Cross. After the debate, Wells and Thomas walked back into the room.

That night, more than 500 people gathered for a dinner to celebrate the anniversary of the BSU. Wells and Thomas sat with Father Brooks at the head table. Jenkins then introduced Wells to give a speech, in which he attempted to put their shared history and Father Brooks's efforts to integrate the college into a wider perspective.

He started, not with the group of young men who were recruited to an unfamiliar place in 1968, but with the history of a country that had embraced slavery to the point where the concept was embedded as an institution in the Constitution. He talked about Holy Cross's early and all-too-brief experience of integration with the admission of the Healy brothers. He spoke movingly of civil rights, of the impact that desegregation and the words of Dr. King had on a boy growing up in Washington.

These men, his friends and brothers at Holy Cross, were the first generation to grow up after the *Brown* decision took effect. A generation that had nurtured hope for change even as the violence and assassinations of the late 1960s brought some of those dreams crashing to the ground. Against this backdrop, Holy Cross had engaged in a noble experiment, led by Father Brooks, to integrate its student body and to return to its multicultural roots. Despite the anger and resentment and miscommunication, they were all working to make the messy transition to a better society. They were all willing to take deeply personal risks to get there, even at the expense of their own education. To Wells, at least, it was no surprise that many of them had gone on to become leaders in different fields. That was what a great education was supposed to do.

What struck Wells was not just how far racial relations in the United States had progressed since 1968, but how much was still left to be done. For that to happen, he said, the world needed more men like Father Brooks, who had the courage and foresight to integrate the college and had stood as a visionary and friend to the black students at Holy Cross. "I love this man," said Wells, prompting the entire room of people to stand up and cheer. As Brooks looked at the men who had worked so hard to carve out their own success and pave the way for others, he had tears in his eyes. The education, he felt, had truly been his.

WHERE THEY ARE TODAY

The Reverend **John E. Brooks** is now president emeritus and Loyola professor of humanities at Holy Cross. During his tenure as president, from 1970 to 1994, Brooks oversaw a substantial expansion in the school's endowment and twenty-three years of balanced budgets while helping to build Holy Cross into one of the country's top liberal arts institutions. He also made Holy Cross a more vibrant center for the arts, playing a key role in the founding of a gallery on campus and a concert hall that now bears his name.

As president, Father Brooks continued to take bold and controversial actions, including the transition to coeducation and his decision in 1986 to make Holy Cross a founding member of what is now the Patriot League. The league, founded on the principle that scholar-athletes would be academically representative of their class instead of recruited specifically for their athletic talents, firmly moved Holy Cross away from high-stakes sports in favor of what Brooks has called a "more balanced" approach. It also eliminated the cherished football rivalry with Boston College.

More important, Brooks has influenced generations of Holy Cross alumni with his vision, compassion, and wisdom. His quiet devotion to God has been an inspiration to many who have found their own vocation, and he is celebrated as a model of the Jesuits' continued commitment to social justice, excellence in teaching, personal, spiritual, and intellectual growth, and the courage to question the status quo. He continues to teach a seminar in Christology and has never relented in his mission to nurture the next generation of leaders.

Stanley Grayson earned a law degree from the University of Michigan in Ann Arbor. While there, he met an undergraduate named Patricia McKinnon; the two married and had two children. After graduation, Grayson went to work in the law department of the Metropolitan Life Insurance Company in New York City. After a few years, he moved into city government, becoming chairman of New York City's Financial Services Corporation. In the late 1980s, under Mayor Ed Koch, Grayson served as the city's finance commissioner and then as deputy mayor for finance and economic development.

Grayson has spent most of his career on Wall Street, first as a vice president at Goldman Sachs and then as a managing director at Prudential Securities, where he headed up the public finance department. Since 2002, he has been president and chief operating officer of M.R. Beal & Company, one of the country's oldest minority-owned investment banks. While Grayson shunned formal roles in the BSU, he has since become very active in public life, serving on the Port Authority Board of Commissioners and on the boards of the March of Dimes, Marymount College, and, of course, Holy Cross.

Gilbert Hardy graduated with distinction from Yale Law School and clerked for U.S. District Court chief judge Almeric Christian for two years in the Virgin Islands before moving to Washington, D.C. He was a partner in the law firm of Wald, Harkrader & Ross when he introduced his colleague Anita Hill to Clarence Thomas, who hired her to work at the Department of Education and later the Equal Employment Opportunity Commission. Hardy had recently started his own law firm when he died at the age of thirty-eight in a scuba-diving accident off the coast of Morocco in August 1989.

Eddie Jenkins's career in the NFL was short-lived but dramatic. After graduation, he immediately became a running back with the Miami Dolphins, who that year became the only team in NFL history to go undefeated for an entire season. After the Dolphins won the 1973 Super Bowl, Jenkins played two more seasons in the NFL before entering Suffolk University Law School in 1975.

Despite his initial dislike of Worcester, Jenkins ended up spending much of his career in Massachusetts. He has worked as a prosecutor, an arbitrator, and a mediator, first joining the U.S. Labor Department before setting up his own practice for fifteen years and running for district attorney and Boston city council, though he was not elected. In 2003, he became chairman of the Massachusetts Alcoholic Beverages Control Commission. He later became director of enforcement at the Registry of Motor Vehicles. Jenkins's son Julian, one of two children from his first marriage, was drafted to play with the Tampa Bay Buccaneers in 2006.

Jenkins is an adjunct professor at Suffolk Law School and a leader in several organizations, including Outward Bound. He ran a youth basketball program at the Roxbury YMCA called No Books, No Balls, which encourages young athletes to keep up with their studies. Jenkins also helped to start a mentoring program for former gang members and was chairman of Urban Edge, a community development corporation that assists small businesses and works to increase affordable housing around Boston. He and his wife live in Boston, where he is currently working on a history of Da'Ville, the Queens neighborhood where he grew up.

Upon graduation, **Edward P. Jones** moved back to Washington to help care for his mother, Jeanette M. Jones, living paycheck to paycheck as he wrote for various publications and worked odd jobs. Shortly after Jeanette died in 1975, Jones sold his first short story to *Essence*. He didn't realize he'd sold it until about fifteen months after the fact because he was homeless at the time. In 1979, he enrolled in graduate school at the University of Virginia to focus on his creative writing, and he received his MFA in 1981. A year later, he found steady work as a proofreader at *Tax Notes,* where he would work for the next two decades.

His first collection of short stories, *Lost in the City,* came out in 1992 and was a finalist for the National Book Award. The book was the realization of Jones's dream: to capture the lives of people in his city as James Joyce had done with the people of Dublin. The book also earned him the PEN/Hemingway Award and the Lannan Literary Award, as well as some prize money that proved helpful when he was laid off from *Tax Notes* in 2002. Living on a combination of savings, his small severance, and unemployment insurance, Jones then sat down to write a story that had been unfolding in his mind since he learned about black slave owners in a class at Holy Cross.

With the publication of *The Known World* in 2003, Jones was hailed as one of the finest writers of his generation. Set in a fictionalized county of antebellum Virginia, the novel revolves around the life of a black slaveholder named Henry Townsend. Jones won the National Book Critics Circle Award and the Pulitzer Prize for fiction in 2004, as well as a $500,000 MacArthur "genius grant." A year later, he won the International IMPAC Dublin Literary Award for the best work of fiction published in English.

In 2006, Jones published another celebrated collection of short stories, *All Aunt Hagar's Children.* In 2009, he was a visiting professor at George Washington University, and he joined the faculty full-time in September 2010. Jones has never married and still lives alone in Washington, D.C.

Arthur Martin moved to Washington to attend Georgetown University's Law School after graduating from Holy Cross in 1970. While there, he became national chairman of what was then called the Black American Law Students Association. Upon graduation, he moved back to New

Jersey, where he eventually became deputy attorney general, specializing in civil rights, and spent two decades in private practice. He is now the director of workplace compliance at the Newark Housing Authority and is a founding trustee of Christ the King Preparatory School in Newark. Martin married his high school sweetheart, Marilyn Herod, three days after graduating from Holy Cross in 1970. They have one son.

The career path of **Clarence Thomas** has been widely chronicled. His experience at Yale University's law school was a disappointment and, he says, led to no job offers at big-city firms, as many assumed he had earned a spot at Yale because he was black. He moved to Missouri, where he became an assistant attorney general, and later moved on to Washington. His first high-profile job was in 1982, when he was appointed chairman of the Equal Employment Opportunity Commission. Two years later, his marriage to Kathy Ambush, with whom he had a son, ended in divorce. He married Virginia Lamp in 1987 and was nominated to the District of Columbia Circuit Court of Appeals in 1990.

About a year later, President George H. W. Bush nominated Thomas to the Supreme Court of the United States. The bitter confirmation hearings, involving allegations of crude behavior and unwanted advances toward former colleague Anita Hill, thrust Thomas into the spotlight. Among the speakers who came to his defense was Father Brooks.

Thomas has since become the most polarizing member of the Court, inspiring passionate reaction from fans and foes alike. While many are quick to note his silence as a Supreme Court Justice—2011 marked the fifth anniversary of the last time he'd asked a question during an oral argument—others argue that Thomas has quietly become an intellectual leader in some of the most critical areas of constitutional law. Along with the many books that examine his life and his record, Thomas himself set out to capture what shaped his philosophy in his memoir, *My Grandfather's Son*. Through it all, he has remained attached to Holy Cross, where he served as a trustee, and to Father Brooks. Despite the isolation and anger and the growing disconnection he eventually felt from some of his peers, Thomas says his Holy Cross years were a time in his life when people seemed to look beyond his skin color and accept him for who he was. The expectation from Father Brooks was that he would work hard and do his best, not that he would think in a certain way. To this day, Holy Cross remains a place where he feels he belongs.

Theodore Wells graduated from Harvard in 1976, with both an MBA from Harvard Business School and a JD from Harvard Law School, where he was an editor of the prestigious *Harvard Civil Rights–Civil Liberties Law Review.* After graduation, he moved to New Jersey, where he served for a year as a law clerk to Judge John J. Gibbons, on the United States Court of Appeals for the Third Circuit, before going into private practice.

He now works in New York City, where he is a partner and the co-chair of the litigation department at Paul, Weiss, Rifkind, Wharton & Garrison LLP, one of the country's premiere corporate law firms. Wells is widely considered to be one of the greatest trial lawyers of his generation, and over the past twenty years various publications have recognized him as one of the most influential lawyers in America. *The National Law Journal* named him Lawyer of the Year in 2006 and one of the decade's most influential lawyers in 2010.

Along with representing Scooter Libby, Dick Cheney's former chief of staff, Wells has successfully defended such high-profile politicians as Secretary of Labor Raymond Donovan, Secretary of Agriculture Michael Espy, New York governor Eliot Spitzer, and New York governor David Paterson. He has represented Wall Street titans including Michael Milken and Frank Quattrone, and major corporations, including Citigroup, which he successfully defended against an $8 billion civil fraud claim.

After graduating from Holy Cross, where he later served as a trustee, Wells continued to devote much of his life to civil rights and political causes. He has served as general counsel to the New Jersey NAACP, state chair of the United Negro College Fund, and co-chair of the board of the NAACP Legal Defense and Educational Fund, as well as treasurer of U.S. senator Bill Bradley's presidential campaign in 2002.

In December 2011, Ted Wells received the prestigious Thurgood Marshall Lifetime Achievement Award from the NAACP Legal Defense and Education Fund for his commitment to civil rights issues. A month later, he celebrated his fortieth wedding anniversary with his wife, Nina, who has had a distinguished career as a practicing lawyer, corporate executive, and public servant, serving four years as secretary of state in New Jersey. They have two children, and Ted's mother, Phyllis, continues to live in the same house in Washington, D.C., where Ted grew up.

ACKNOWLEDGMENTS

First, I'd like to thank the men whose college lives were chronicled in this book: Stan Grayson, Eddie Jenkins, Edward P. Jones, Clarence Thomas, and Ted Wells. They are not men who need or seek the spotlight, but because of their gratitude to Father Brooks, all of them were generous with their time and insights to help make the story accurate.

I'm grateful to the many other alumni and faculty, named and unnamed, who also opened up about their lives during that period. They include Art Martin, Jaffe Dickerson, Malcolm Joseph, Walter Roy, Joe Wilson, Gordon Davis, Orion Douglass, Bob DeShay, Jim Gallagher, Dennis Golden, Tom Anderson, John Siraco, Ron Lawson, Lenny Cooper, Bob Credle, Ogretta McNeil, and John Dorenkamp, to name a few. I am also grateful to the many others who knew the men and who were equally critical to my reporting, from Phyllis Wells and Nina Mitchell to Leland Hardy (Gil Hardy's brother) and Vivianne Townes (Gil's girlfriend and later wife).

Mark Savolis and his team at the Holy Cross Archives were very helpful when I was researching the book, and Ellen Ryder, the college's dynamic director of public affairs, was my guiding light on campus. The Reverend Michael C. McFarland, S.J., who recently stepped down as president, was among the many in the Holy Cross community who made this book possible.

Thanks to Eric Starkman, who introduced me to Stan Grayson. Paul Barrett, Mike France, and Steve Adler then helped me shape the story into a feature for *BusinessWeek,* and my agent Mark Reiter who saw its potential as a book. Cindy Spiegel, the incredible editor whose imprint bears her name, was willing to take that bet. I can't tell her how grateful I am for her patience, intelligence, and good humor through this effort. I also thank Hana Landes and Laura Van der Veer for their amazing work.

I had great advice from David Breskin and from my sisters Shirley and Elise Brady. Thanks are also due to my editors at *Businessweek*—Josh Tyrangiel, Norm Pearlstine, and Ellen Pollock—who offered up time and encouragement. And my family bore the greatest burden of this project. Thank you, Elliott, Natalie, and Connor: Your encouragement, love, and understanding helped me to get this done. Thank you, Barry, for being there to root for me and carry the load without complaint. I love you.

Finally, I'd like to express my gratitude to Father Brooks. It has been an honor to get to know him through this process, and to witness the profound impact that one man can have on the lives of those around him.

NOTES

INTRODUCTION

1 **one of the best:** "A Libby Lawyer Long Used to the Legal Spotlight," *New York Times,* November 5, 2005.

4 **memoirs of Justice Clarence Thomas:** Clarence Thomas, *My Grandfather's Son* (New York: HarperCollins, 2007), pp. 49–65.

CHAPTER 1: ALL OF KING'S MEN

9 **bold and inclusive vision:** Giuseppe Alberigo, *A Brief History of Vatican II,* trans. Matthew Sherry (Maryknoll, N.Y.: Orbis Books, 2005).

9 **the silence haunted him:** Thomas, *My Grandfather's Son,* p. 42.

15 **brutal slaying:** *CBS Evening News with Walter Cronkite,* April 4, 1968, www.youtube.com/watch?v=cmOBbxgxKvo (accessed September 8, 2011).

18 **Emotions were running high:** Joseph E. Peniel, *Waiting 'Til the Midnight Hour: A Narrative History of Black Power in America* (New York: Henry Holt, 2006), pp. 227–28.

18 **By Sunday morning:** "People Were Out of Control: Remembering the 1968 Riots," *Washingtonian,* April 1, 2008.

19 **$322,000 for each enemy killed:** *Eyes on the Prize: America's Civil Rights Movement,* vol. 5, *The Promised Land (1967–68), American Experience* on PBS, King on the war on poverty.

19 **blacks have actually been in jail:** Ibid., interview between Muhammad Ali and Bud Collins.

CHAPTER 2: AGAINST THE CLOCK

23 **Afro-Americans:** "Interview with New Dean Probes Contemporary Issues," *Crusader,* September 20, 1968.

26 **courage, conviction and eloquence:** Anthony J. Kuzniewski, S.J., *Thy Honored Name: A History of The College of the Holy Cross, 1843–1994* (Washington, D.C.: Catholic University of America Press, 1999), p. 392.

29 **I'm happy tonight:** Martin Luther King, Jr., "I've Been to the Mountaintop" speech, Memphis, April 3, 1968, www.americanrhetoric.com/speeches/mlkivebeentothemountaintop.htm (accessed September 8, 2011).

CHAPTER 3: FIRST IMPRESSIONS

34 **the imprisonment of men's souls:** "To Mr. and Mrs. Yesterday," *New York Times,* March 24, 1968.

46 **He had shamed the family:** Thomas, *My Grandfather's Son,* p. 45.

48 **He was stuck:** Ibid., p. 46.

CHAPTER 4: COME TOGETHER

50 **poor and the oppressed:** "Interview with New Dean," *Crusader,* September 20, 1968.

52 **The incoming generation:** Nineteen sixty-eight marked the height of troop levels in Vietnam. See www.heritage.org/research/nationalsecurity/cda04–11.cfm.

52 **The rest were an eclectic mix:** College of the Holy Cross Archives & Special Collections, Rev. John E. Brooks, S.J., Papers.

53   **scale its athletic program:** "A. D. Litte Report Recommends Athletic Scholarship Abolition," *Crusader,* May 8, 1970.

53   **average SAT scores of athletes:** Holy Cross Archives.

CHAPTER 5: WINDS OF CHANGE

67   **there is not one:** Kuzniewski, *Thy Honored Name,* p. 25.

68   **take over the world:** Jack Tager, *Boston Riots: Three Centuries of Social Violence* (Boston: Northeastern University Press, 2000), pp. 118–19.

68   **financial cost of maintaining slave families:** Thomas J. Murphy, *Jesuit Slaveholding in Maryland, 1717–1838* (New York: Routledge, 2001), p. 216.

69   **275,000 black undergraduates:** "Black Mood on Campus," *Newsweek,* February 10, 1968.

70   **populated by the failures:** Michael Harrington, *The Other America: Poverty in the United States* (New York: Macmillan, 1962), p. 10.

73   **Thomas got up and walked out:** Thomas, *My Grandfather's Son,* p. 50.

80   **admit their ignorance:** Holy Cross Archives, Brooks Papers.

81   **running scared:** Ibid.

CHAPTER 6: LOVE, LIBERTY, AND LEARNING

87   **dirtying up:** Holy Cross Archives, BSU Papers.

93   **The cost of war:** Bruce O. Solheim, *The Vietnam War Era: A Personal Journey* (Lincoln: University of Nebraska Press, 2006), p. 49.

95   **for personal reasons:** "Boisture Quits Holy Cross," *Boston Herald Traveler,* December 12, 1968.

97   **I cared for her:** Edward P. Jones, "Shacks," *The New Yorker,* June 13, 2011.

99   **White racism:** *Worcester Evening Gazette,* December 31, 1969 (reprinted in "Blacks Charge Unconscious White Racism," *Crossroads,* November 1970).

106   **a degree of suspicion:** "Situation of Blacks at Holy Cross Analyzed," *Crusader,* April 25, 1969.

107   **an ignorant illiterate:** Thomas, *My Grandfather's Son,* p. 53.

CHAPTER 7: BLACK POWER AND A LOST SEASON

110 **If Holy Cross doesn't get these students:** "Blacks Discuss Change with President Swords," *Crusader,* February 28, 1968.

112 **totally alien:** Holy Cross Archives, Brooks Papers.

112 **The fact is:** Ibid.

113 **which is not revolutionary:** "The Case for Separatism: 'Black Perspective,'" *Newsweek,* February 10, 1969.

113 **foisted on them:** "The Case Against Separatism: 'Black Jim Crow,'" *Newsweek,* February 10, 1969.

113 **freshmen we brought in:** As he told one newspaper reporter at the *Worcester Telegram*, the "freshmen we brought in measure up in all ways. They are strong personalities and have not folded under some tremendous psychological and social pressures."

115 **in all fairness and justice:** Holy Cross Archives, Brooks Papers.

116 **A black man:** "Fr. Swords: Integrationist Leadership Lacking," *Crusader,* February 28, 1968.

116 **opportunity for an increased social life:** Holy Cross Archives, BSU Papers.

118 **one of HC's best:** *Crossroads,* January 1970. See also: "HC Offense Looks Strong, Defense Could Be Shaky," *The Crusader,* September 19, 1969.

118 **his father, Hipolit Moncevicz:** "HC Football has soared, sunk to depths," *Worcester Telegram & Gazette,* September 24, 1995.

119 **The Harvard team:** "Harvard Subdues Holy Cross, 13–0, Extending Unbeaten String to Ten," *New York Times,* September 28, 1969.

121 **been forced to cancel:** "Holy Cross Cancels Football as Hepatitis Strikes Squad," *New York Times,* October 7, 1969.

121 ***The Journal:*** "The Holy Cross College Football Team Hepatitis Outbreak," *Journal of the American Medical Association* 219 (February 1972): 706–8.

CHAPTER 8: FREEDOM AND WAR

125 **They sometimes delighted in the crude:** Also chronicled in a book by Jane Mayer and Jill Abramson, *Strange Justice: The Selling of Clarence Thomas* (Boston: Houghton Mifflin, 1994).

132 **rising as the wheel rises:** Clarence Thomas, "Education: The Second Door to Freedom," speech to College of the Holy Cross, February 3, 1994.

132 **relax and be magnanimous:** "Magnanimity," *Crusader,* March 2, 1970.

133 **I suggest you explain:** Holy Cross Archives, Brooks Papers.

133 **Old Black Joe:** Kuzniewski, *Thy Honored Name,* p. 413.

133 **He had bought a typewriter:** "The Column: Have to Get Guns and Be Men," *Crusader,* May 1, 1970.

135 **just like a nigger!:** Lew Alcindor, "My Story," *Sports Illustrated,* October 27, 1969.

137 **the black man's philosophy:** Holy Cross Archives, BSU Papers.

138 **I ain't got no quarrel:** "Muhammad Ali: The Greatest," *Time,* June 14, 1999.

CHAPTER 9: THE WALKOUT

141 **Opposition to the war:** "Who Killed Thai Khac Chuyen? Not I, Said the CIA," *Time,* September 5, 1969.

145 **a much higher issue:** "Initial BSU Statement on Board Report," *Crusader,* December 19, 1969.

146 **no alternative except to take action:** Ibid.

157 **if you let these men quit:** Holy Cross Archives, BSU Papers.

158 **courage:** "Courage at Holy Cross," *Worcester Telegram,* December 13, 1969.

159 **I am granting amnesty:** Holy Cross Archives, Brooks Papers; "Holy Cross President Reinstates 16 Students Suspended in Protest," *Worcester Telegram,* December 15, 1969.

CHAPTER 10: WHAT DO YOU FIGHT FOR?

161 **A businessman propped a casket:** "The Death of Free Enterprise," *Worcester Telegram,* December 20, 1969.

166 **Clarence has a cumulative quality point index:** Holy Cross Archives, Brooks Papers.

170 **This must be the nigger contingent:** Thomas, *My Grandfather's Son,* p. 59.

173   **minimum-security penitentiary:** "Yippee leader Hoffman attacks injustices in American society," *Crusader,* April 10, 1970.

175   **While 55 percent of Americans:** Joseph Carroll, Gallup poll, "The Iraq-Vietnam Comparison," June 15, 2004, www.gallup.com/poll/11998/iraqvietnam_comparison.aspx (accessed September 8, 2011).

175   **A few days later:** University of Georgia, www.civilrights.uga.edu/cities/augusta/governor_visits.htm (accessed September 8, 2011).

175   **On May 14, police opened fire:** may41970.com/Jackson%20State/jackson_state_may_1970.htm (accessed September 8, 2011).

175   **catalytic events:** Swords's commencement address, Holy Cross, 1970.

176   **convinced the Administration:** Holy Cross Archives, BSU Papers.

CHAPTER 11: EYES ON THE PRIZE

179   **one of Brooks's first acts:** "Holy Cross Plans to Admit Women," *New York Times,* January 12, 1971. "The Holy Cross decision makes it the last of the Jesuits' 28 American colleges and universities to become co-educational."

182   **The anarchist priest:** "Vietnam and Holy Cross: A Timeline," *Holy Cross Magzine,* April 1999.

183   **who had supported and pushed:** William Van Etten Casey, S.J., and Philip Nobile, eds., *The Berrigans* (New York: Avon Books, 1971), p. 9.

183   **the cradle of the Catholic Left:** "Rebel Priests: The Curious Case of the Berrigans," *Time,* January 25, 1971.

184   **security officers were following her around:** "All's Wells," *Suffolk Law,* Spring 2008.

186   **When the BSU van broke down:** Holy Cross Archives, Brooks Papers.

187   **I am very much aware:** Holy Cross Archives, Brooks Papers.

188   **all the tools for stardom:** "Crusaders Inexperienced; Defense Looks Impressive," *Crusader,* September 25, 1970.

188   **Still, in the second game:** "Boston U. Downs Holy Cross, 33–23," *New York Times,* October 18, 1970.

189   **I leave with no ill feeling:** "Whitton Submits Resignation; Reasons Are Health and Family," *Crusader,* February 12, 1971.

190 **the most underrated performer:** "Talented Purple Cagers Boast Experience, Depth," *Crusader,* November 20, 1970.

190 **Stan was great:** "Grayson on Erving: 'The Best I've Faced,'" *Crusader,* February 5, 1971.

191 **That's nice, son:** Thomas, *My Grandfather's Son,* p. 95.

CHAPTER 12: MOVING ON

194 **gung ho attitude:** "Holy Cross Ends Slump in 21–6 Harvard Upset," *New York Times,* September 26, 1971.

195 **He was feeling more assertive:** Mike Hickey, *Dream Big Dreams: The Jack Donohue Story* (Maya Publishing, 2006), p. 141.

198 **petty and characteristically racist:** Holy Cross Archives, Brooks Papers.

200 **The black community at Holy Cross:** "Blacks Take Over Fenwick Complex," *Crusader,* May 5, 1972.

201 **genuine regret:** Ibid.

203 **may be the most popular student:** " '72 'Crusader of the Year' Who Else but Stan Grayson," *Crusader,* April 14, 1972.

WHERE THEY ARE TODAY

217 **While many are quick:** "Partners," *The New Yorker,* August 29, 2011.

INDEX

ABOUT THE AUTHOR

DIANE BRADY grew up in Scotland and Canada before moving to Nairobi to begin her career as a journalist. She now writes for *Bloomberg Businessweek* in New York City, where she lives with her husband and three children. This is her first book.

ABOUT THE TYPE

This book was set in Minion, a 1990 Adobe Originals typeface by Robert Slimbach. Minion is inspired by classical, old-style typefaces of the late Renaissance, a period of elegant, beautiful, and highly readable type designs. Created primarily for text setting, Minion combines the aesthetic and functional qualities that make text type highly readable with the versatility of digital technology.